SIX PERCENT

SIX PERCENT
DAVE JACKA

PUBLISHING

Published by Dirt Track Publishing
PO Box 208
Fairfield Vic 3078
Australia

Copyright © Dave Jacka 2019
Dave Jacka asserts his right to be known as the author of this work.

ALL RIGHTS RESERVED.
No part of this book may be reproduced, stored in a retrieval system, transmitted in any form by any means electronic, mechanical, photocopying, recording or otherwise without prior written consent of the publishers.
All inquiries should be made to the author.

 A catalogue record for this book is available from the National Library of Australia

9780648582601 (paperback)
9780648582618 (ebook)

Cover design by Peter Long
Cover photos: Dave Jacka photo by Andrew Raszevski
Flying Trike photo by The Border Mail
Text design by Libby Austen
Illustrations by Karen Rumley

This book is dedicated to my parents, Brian and Roberta Jacka, and to my sisters Kathryn, Marguerite, Elizabeth (EJ) and Madeleine. It is their love and support that helped me get through my darkest days and go on to live a challenging and fulfilling life for which I am truly grateful.

CONTENTS

Introduction 1
Prologue 5

FIRST LIFE
1 The Last Night 11

SECOND LIFE
2 Change in Destiny 19
3 Intensive Care 23
4 13 East 33
5 Pale-Blue Wall 49
6 First Day 53
7 New Wheels 63
8 Occupational Torture 69
9 First Outing 73
10 Manhood 79
11 An Idle Mind Is the Devil's Workshop 81
12 Confronting 85
13 Siberia 89
14 Breaking Out 93
15 Little Goals = Hope 101
16 Day Visits 107
17 Goodbye 17 111
18 Transition 117
19 Home 133

20	Back Behind the Wheel	149
21	Trying New Things	157
22	Crossroad	163
23	True Potential	173

THIRD LIFE

24	Rebuilding My Life	179
25	World Championships	185
26	A Job	191
27	Paralympics	195

FOURTH LIFE

28	My Home	209
29	Moving Forward	217
30	The Seed	223
31	Disappointment	231
32	Hope	235
33	Who Will Help Me?	239
34	Solo	245
35	After Solo	253
36	Final Thoughts	255
	Epilogue	257
	Acknowledgements	259

INTRODUCTION

Late one evening, as I was getting out of my car, my wheelchair rolled away and all I could do was watch it gather speed down a steep incline. Being alone, I had no option but to chase it downhill in my car, then manoeuvre the vehicle like a bulldozer, pushing the wheelchair up to a flat spot for another attempt at getting out of my car.

When I told people this story, and many others about learning to live with my disability, I would usually get a few laughs; but some people would also suggest, 'Dave, you should write a book!'

To be honest, initially I didn't think I had a story that was unique enough to be worth telling; nor did I think I could possibly write a book. At school I disliked English; actually, for that matter, I simply disliked school. My identity at nineteen years old, before my accident, was defined by my physical capabilities—my job as a carpenter, going out with my mates and my passions of surfing and snow-skiing.

However, following the motorbike accident that left me with a broken neck and quadriplegia with only six percent function, the world as I knew it was gone forever. Ever so slowly, I had to rebuild my life and, most importantly, to redefine who I was. Being unable to do the physical things I once took for granted forced me to seek different solutions—to relearn how to do many basic tasks such as feeding myself, putting on a jumper, using a pen or getting myself in and out of my wheelchair.

This relearning process, as hard and excruciatingly frustrating as it was, brought about significant changes within me. I developed a new mindset, a new perception of what I was capable of. I began to see challenges as possibilities, not impossibilities—and that my potential was limited only by what I believed.

This led me to see that a disability does not define who you are or what you can achieve. Just because you can't do something the way you did it previously does not mean you can't do it. When I opened my mind to other possibilities, when I thought outside the square, I revived a lost dream I'd had since I was a small boy—my dream to fly.

Many considered this to be impossible; in fact, other people's negativity became a greater barrier to me than my physical ones. But I was fortunate to find one instructor who could look beyond my disability and who believed in me. In 2006, he helped me achieve my impossible dream: I learned to fly.

It wasn't until 2013, after my solo flight around Australia, that many people who were interested in my story affirmed the idea that I should write a book. Given all I had experienced over the last twenty-five years, I now felt that I did, in fact, have a story to tell; but equally, given my early dislike for English and schooling, it was a challenge I couldn't let pass!

I titled this book *Six Percent* because early on after my accident, a specialist told me that I was 94 percent impaired, which meant that only around six percent of my body was still working. This number stuck in my mind, and it left me with a nagging question: *What does six percent actually mean?* If only six percent of my muscles work, what does that mean for my life? Does it mean I would only have six percent of a life? Would I have only six percent of enjoyment, or be able to do just six percent of what I had done previously? This question of what I would be able to do and experience with

INTRODUCTION

six percent was ever-present in my mind. I was the only person who could answer it.

Six Percent is the story of how I rebuilt my life following my accident. It traces the gradual change in my understanding of what was possible—from being diagnosed with quadriplegia with little hope for the future, to chasing my boyhood dream of learning to fly.

In writing this book, some names have been changed to protect identities. I have recalled many details, including characters dialogue from memory, so please forgive any inaccuracies. The story is from my perspective, describing how I saw the events, and I have been honest and open about what I experienced and what was going on in my mind as I learned to deal with my new life. Some may say I've been too open and, to be honest, I have questioned this myself and feel a bit nervous about other people hovering a magnifying glass over aspects of my life.

But if I skimmed over the parts that were difficult, regretful, embarrassing or confronting, I would not be providing the reader with a true perspective of what people in similar situations have to go through to come out the other side.

Over the years I have had to devise many strategies to overcome problems and challenges. Many solutions have been my own, but I also got some or parts of ideas from others, whether through sport or daily life. By adapting these ideas to my own circumstances, I managed to overcome the barriers to achieving my goals. I hope that through sharing my experiences, trials and triumphs, others may find some ideas on how to tackle problems, and thereby add value to their lives.

Also, I hope that people with limited understanding of disability may gain insight into some of the challenges we have to deal with each day. Life can change in an instant, whether due to an accident or illness. Having others' support and understanding can make a world of difference in helping people adjust to big life changes. I also hope that with this insight, people might become a little more open and accepting; not be as quick to judge, and give people with disabilities a fair go.

Lastly, I hope readers find my story entertaining. Although many of my experiences were difficult, particularly in the early years, when I look back on them, I see the humour. I have tried to reflect this in my writing.

PROLOGUE

Bright fluorescent lights reflected off the scuffed stainless-steel walls around me, the musty smell indicating that few people came this way through the old abandoned wing of the Austin Hospital.

Bang! The lift jerked, shuddering to an abrupt stop. The doors rattled as they opened, revealing a dark, empty passage that led to my new home for the next six months.

It was a stark contrast to the relatively modern hospital building of the acute ward in 13 East. The high ceilings and arches in the wide passage, the thick brick walls separating large rooms, four beds in each, hinted at a bygone Victorian era.

Sally, a nurse, pushed my creaking, lumbering beast to the brightly lit nurses' station. The duty nurse turned around, smiled at me and continued to sort through some folders.

'You must be David. We have your room set up,' she said. 'Jackie will be with you soon to help you unpack. It's just down there on the left,' she said, momentarily pausing from her important sorting process to point down the hall.

My wheelchair was more like a Jason Recliner sofa chair on wheels. Sally was strong for her size, heaving it around and pushing me towards my room.

There were no windows in my new home. White fluorescent lights hung off the high ceilings, making the room glow like the inside of a fish 'n' chip shop. In each corner of the room a bed was pushed against the wall, a light-blue curtain separating each quarter for privacy. Unlike the room in 13 East where I had spent the last two months, with its multitude of hoses and fittings jutting out of the walls and TVs above the beds, this room was bare. Just a bed and bedhead, and a chrome metal frame suspending a sling over the bed, to give the patient something to grab hold of when sitting up or rolling over—or, for those who felt they had nothing left in life, to hang themselves (with a bit of ingenuity).

The room was empty, as the other three patients were out. 'I'll leave you here, Dave. Someone will be with you soon,' said Sally, placing a warm hand on my shoulder. 'I'll drop by soon to see how you are.' Her soft smile reassured me.

'You still have to bring in the curry you promised me, Sal,' I chided.

'See ya, Dave,' she said, as the squeak of her rubber-soled shoes faded behind me.

The faint noises of other people drifted down the corridor; their rooms seemed so far away. I sat motionless; I was trapped in a paralysed body in the middle of the room, unable to budge the huge wheelchair with my weak, spindly arms. I couldn't look around as the neck brace held my head firm like a clamp to protect my weak neck. I could only sit and stare at the bare pale-blue wall in front of me.

As the minutes ticked by an overwhelming feeling of emptiness, then despair, began to rise in my chest. I forced myself to take deep breaths, but the wave of desperation and hopelessness was so powerful, it flattened what was left of my wavering spirit.

Tears began to trickle, then gush, down my cheeks as my will to hold back my emotions failed like a dam breach. A stream of water cascaded down my face into my neck brace, which soaked it up like a sponge. My internal voice was screaming, but no sound came out of my mouth. The overwhelming despair gagged my soul. I felt so helplessly lost.

In that moment, as if I had been slammed by a road train, it suddenly dawned on me that I couldn't do anything except sit there and stare at the pale-blue wall. I now understood what quadriplegia meant. I was helpless. My dreams, my life, my world, my future, were gone.

FIRST LIFE

1
THE LAST NIGHT

I was really looking forward to going out and catching up with my mates. It being a Saturday, I worked only a half day, a welcome change from the six full days I'd been doing on the Sportscraft job in the city fitting out two floors.

I had been working for John 'S'—he had one of those unpronounceable Polish surnames—over the last six months, since January 1988. He was a really nice guy, fairly laid-back; this was probably due to the occasional joint he and his sidekick enjoyed. John was a builder and much of his work was with Sportscraft, the clothing manufacturer in Hawthorn, doing maintenance at the various sites, particularly joinery work building shelving, cupboards and display stands.

I was in my third year as an apprentice carpenter, and I loved what I did. I could never draw freehand or paint in art class, but when it came to making or building things, I was a natural. What I envisioned came out through my hands. I couldn't sculpt, but by adding a piece here and there, I could build something. In Grade 1, I stuck a few pieces of wood together that faintly resembled a plane and all the other kids, mad on planes as I was, wanted to play with it.

Also, I loved being outside and creating things, where at the end of the day I could stand back and see the effort I had put in. I liked the hard-physical work: it made me feel as though I'd accomplished something. At six-foot-three, well-built and strong, I excelled in the heavy work which kept me fit for surfing, and for my biggest passion, snow-skiing.

I enjoyed working in the city but even if I left home at 6.30 a.m., it took me well over an hour on the South Eastern carpark/freeway to get to the Sportscraft job. I envied the motorbike riders darting between cars jammed bumper to bumper, stopping only at the lights, getting to the front, and then being the first off, rocketing into the distance.

I had always wanted to get a motorbike. When I was seven or eight, my best mate Pete and I would head down to the local tip on a Saturday and watch the motocross riders race around the dirt track, the two-stroke engines screaming and flicking mud onto us as they went past. It was awesome! I dreamt of getting a Yamaha YZ80 and racing around the track one day, kitted up in my cool battle gear. It was a thrill to be asked by a rider to hold his bike while he went off to do something important, like taking a piss. When we came back to reality, deflated from not knowing how we could ever save up enough money to buy one, we'd head off to the tip and scavenge, bringing home a treasure trove of great stuff, from soft-drink bottles which fetched a whopping 20 cents each, to lawn mowers that occasionally worked, and lots of junk that Dad invariably took back weeks later.

In my early teens, I looked forward to visiting the dairy farm of my uncle and aunty near Camperdown where I rode their Honda CT 125 motorbike in the back paddocks, splattering liquid cow shit over my legs, with the occasional drop flicking onto my face—it was best to keep your lips tightly shut.

My sister Elizabeth, or EJ as she likes to be called, who was number three in our family of five kids (with me being number four), had a second-hand silver Honda CB 250. She rarely rode and was happy for me to use it. The idea of never getting caught in stationary traffic on the freeway again really appealed to me, and I pictured myself looking cool on the bike. I decided to sit the riding test and get my learner's permit.

I showed up on the nominated day, listened to some theory, watched a video, did a multiple-choice test; then, with some tips from the instructor and a little practice riding around a carpark, I passed the practical test, which gave me my learner's in March 1988. The last thing the tester said to the group was, 'Don't become a statistic!' *Not a chance*, I thought.

With little money to my name, I had to forgo the flash leather bike jacket for the moment; instead, I donned my grey and pink ski jacket, ski gloves and work boots and hit the roads, taking the bike everywhere. Being a four-stroke 250cc it was a little slow, but with the wind behind me and in a crouched position I could get it up to 110 km/hr at a push—which felt very fast. I loved riding around the winding roads up in the Dandenong Ranges, getting it down low on its side, accelerating out of the corners, the back tyre just holding on. It was exhilarating.

'You're a risk-taker,' Tanya, my girlfriend at the time, would say with obvious disapproval as I slid the back end of my old Ford Falcon XW around a corner in the wet. I had always been willing to push the limits, usually further than most of my friends. As kids, we all liked the adrenalin rush, whether it was racing our billy-carts down the street, sliding them out and crashing into gutters, taking some skin off in the process; or jumping our bikes over an obstacle or seeing how far we could fly without crashing. When someone made a jump, I wanted to beat it. Maybe it was my competitive spirit? With the advantage of being taller and stronger than all my mates, and willing to push it, I would take a longer run up for speed and launch myself into the unknown, like a missile. The feeling of weightlessness in slow motion for an instant, just before time sped up as I landed hard, skidding to a stop on my BMX, gave me the biggest thrill.

Growing up, my family spent many summers at Philip Island. With surf beaches not far away, the allure of surfing was ever-present in my mind. However, as Mum was very risk-averse, she said, 'David, when you can swim five miles, you can learn to surf.' Well, I didn't like swimming, and five miles seemed an awfully long way, so I never pursued it. It was only when I was eighteen and owned a car that I became captivated by the exhilaration of surfing, having first experienced it on a road trip to Port Macquarie with my mates Pete and Mick. From then on, many weekends were spent riding waves in southern Victoria.

But skiing was what I loved most. I learnt the skills when I was eight years old when my family lived in Oregon, USA, for a year while Dad completed his doctorate degree in psychology at the University of Oregon. Eugene is a university town, the home of the green and gold Mighty Ducks. It sits in a valley surrounded by green tree-covered hills, except for winter when it is white with snow. Being close to the ski resorts, I got the rare opportunity to experience a sport I loved: downhill skiing. Without fear, I took to it like a politician does to breaking promises. And hurtling straight down the runs, eyes watering, blasting past uncoordinated beginners, was very exciting. I loved the adrenalin rush, taking risks and getting away with them.

Over the following years Dad would take us kids skiing at Mount Buller for the occasional weekend. I couldn't get enough of it. With gravity hurtling me down the mountain, legs pumping like shock absorbers over moguls, teetering in and out of control, it was so exhilarating.

As with surfing and snow-skiing, riding the motorbike gave me a tremendous sense of freedom. Sitting on a machine, holding on tight and accelerating as I rolled back the throttle, my body pulled along as I changed up the gears, getting faster and faster, I felt so alive.

There was no plan for where we were going out on the Saturday night. From memory, although this is all quite vague, a few of us—I think it was my mates Pete, Macca and I—met up at Johnny's place. Our usual Saturday nights were spent either going into the city to the Grain Store Tavern, with three levels playing the best of '80s music; or to the Stage 1 Nightclub; or to a local pub to see a band.

We eventually decided to head out to Stage 1 at the Manhattan Hotel in Ringwood with its signature revolving dance floor.

Dressed in our finest nightclub gear—shiny black shirt, thin leather tie, shiny silver pants with big pleats, black pointy-toed shoes and clean underwear—we'd hit the dance floor like it was *Saturday Night Fever*, laying on our best moves that more likely resembled fighting off killer bees while clawing out of a web of elastic bands, all to the latest '80s tunes. This was, of course, a carefully planned strategy to impress the ladies, invariably inviting looks of, 'Is there something wrong with you?' rather than success. Possibly out of pity, a few girls usually did dance with us. By 1 a.m., if the hot dog man wasn't around, we would munch on packets of Cheese Twisties, trying to get one of the few taxies. However, many times it was either a hitchhike or a long, cold walk home.

This night we were in luck: we scored a taxi and headed to Macca's house just around the corner from where I lived, about a five-minute walk.

We arrived at Macca's around 2 a.m. We talked, watched *Rage* and finished off the last of our cigarettes.

Double-checking that no one was holding out, a little panic set in with the thought of spending the rest of the evening without smokes. Ideas on how to get more revolved like a Ferris wheel, the conversation going something like:

'Ok, let's walk up?'

'Na, too far!'

'How about a taxi?'

'Nope, no money left, just enough for the smokes.'

'OK, I'll go home, get the bike and go up to the 7-Eleven for the smokes,' I said. There were no objections, as far as I can remember.

When I make up my mind, I usually follow through, and this was no exception. Also, my mates were relying on me to get the smokes.

About 2.40 a.m., I walked home in the cold, damp night air. It was the middle of winter and I was freezing. I put my hands in my pockets, holding my arms close to my body, trying to keep warm. At 2.50 a.m., I got to my room and fumbled around in the dark, eventually finding the motorbike keys on my desk. I grabbed my new expensive leather riding jacket and helmet, and quietly snuck out the door without disturbing anyone.

Putting my helmet and jacket on, I straddled the bike, pushing it forward to get it off the stand. It being so late at night, and always neighbour conscious, I clicked the gear into neutral and rolled silently down the drive, turning right down my street, Guinevere Parade. Rolling in the silence, the headlight illuminating the road ahead, the glow of the red and green ignition lights on the speedo seemed overly bright in the dark. Flicking off the kill switch, I pressed the starter button, and the high-pitched whir of the starter motor broke the silence. As I rolled the throttle back slightly to feed the engine, the street exploded from dark silence to the muffled grumble of a lion's roar. My left hand pulled the clutch in, my left foot clicked the gear down one, and the engine roared a little louder, telling me it was time for my journey.

I let the clutch out and rolled back the throttle. The bike pulled away, quickly gathering speed, with the cold air chilling my neck.

10 July 1988, 2.56 a.m., marked the last day of my first life, and the first day of my second life.

SECOND LIFE

2

CHANGE IN DESTINY

A woman (I don't know her name) had just got into bed after picking up her daughter from a night out. Without taking too much notice, she heard the rumbling of a motorbike getting louder, then suddenly stop. Coming from a motorbike family, it seemed a little strange, so she asked her husband to take a look outside to see if there was anything wrong.

Rounding the street corner, under the cold glow of the streetlight, he saw the dark outline of a lifeless body on the nature strip in front of a small tree, with a motorbike on its side.

Fuck, I can't breathe. My mind was racing, trying to make sense of what had happened as I suddenly woke up, lying on my side.

'Are you all right?' a soft male voice said from behind me.

'I can't breathe,' I said, thinking the helmet was suffocating me.

'I'll get some scissors to cut the strap off,' said the male voice.

'You'd better call an ambulance,' said a concerned female voice.

I was scared. Male voice cut the strap to my helmet and took it off, but it didn't make any difference to my breathing. I drifted in and out of consciousness. The male voice asked where I lived and my phone number. Surprisingly, I was lucid enough to give him all the details.

My dad was sound asleep and woke hearing the phone ring.

He gathered from what was said that I had had an accident, but mistakenly thought he heard that it was not serious—so, with no great hurry, he put on some warm clothes and drove around the street to find the ambulance staff bending over me on the nature strip. From the way the paramedics were handling me, he soon realised it was more serious than he'd originally understood. They told him they were worried my neck was broken.

I woke up again, more voices around me this time. I was being moved. I heard my dad's voice. As I was lifted, I tried to yell, 'I love you.' Only a whisper came out. I was terrified. Was I going to die? What had happened to me? *I've really fucked up!* I thought.

My memory is more like a TV show: I see the scene as if I'm outside my body, standing back watching the people around me load me into the ambulance. I know I'm awake, it's not a dream. I'm there, and I'm so scared.

As I was loaded into the ambulance, an upside-down face appeared above me; it was the paramedic. 'You'll be all right, mate,' he said reassuringly. I couldn't feel any part of my body except for warm tears streaming down the sides of my temples.

My whole body was paralysed; the chest muscles I needed to breathe weren't working. I had been thrown headfirst into a little tree, shattering the fifth vertebrae in my neck. I was seriously rooted.

Dad came with me in the ambulance to Dandenong Hospital and Mum drove the car there. I can't imagine what they must have been experiencing as their only son, paralysed, was carted away in an ambulance. Not that I can remember, but Dad said that on the way to Dandenong Hospital I was fully conscious. Of the things we talked about, the one thing that still sticks in his mind is my comment that I could not move my arms—and my big worry that I would not be able to do my job as a carpenter without them.

Constantly drifting in and out of consciousness, it was a quick trip to the hospital for me. I sensed people around me making a lot of noise.

'David, we're going to cut your clothes off,' someone told me.

'No, not my new jacket,' I mumbled. But it didn't matter; I couldn't stay awake to argue.

After my examination, the doctors told my parents that I had broken my neck and would be a quadriplegic for the rest of my life. My parents reeled from the shock of the news—their son incapacitated, in a wheelchair, his life's ambitions cut short.

'He won't die here,' the nurse told my parents. Mum thought this was a strange thing to say, as she hadn't even considered that I would die. Dandenong lacked the necessary facilities, so I was transported to the Austin Hospital Spinal Unit where I would be properly looked after—although I have no recollection of the journey. Dad, who again travelled in the ambulance with me, said that twice the ambulance had to stop because the paramedic couldn't find my pulse, it was so weak. It was a tense time for my parents, wondering whether I would get there alive.

My next memory is of waking up, saying to Dad, 'I want to go home.'

'You'll be in hospital for a while,' he said.

I'm not sure when I realised what my injury was. All I can remember is asking Dad in my murky haze of consciousness, 'I'm a quadriplegic, aren't I?'

'Yes,' he replied.

Dad said later that my biggest fear at the time was whether my face would change. I had no idea what quadriplegia was, or what it meant for how I'd look.

It was just four days before my twentieth birthday. In an instant, with one decision, my life had changed completely and irreversibly. I didn't know what would happen to me or whether I would even have a life worth living.

3

INTENSIVE CARE

My memory of that first week is very vague. With the oxygen levels in my blood very low, I was moved to the Intensive Care Unit (ICU).

Glimpsing me in the ICU, anyone could have been forgiven for thinking I was in a medieval torture chamber. My paralysed body was spread out on the bed, arms in the crucifix position. Head tongs that looked like a C-shaped clamp were screwed into the sides of my skull. The tungsten-tipped bolts penetrated the skin and tightened until they bit into my skull sufficiently to allow a rope to be attached with six pounds of weight hanging over the end of the bed, pulling my neck straight, allowing the vertebrae in my neck to heal. The arterial IV plugged into my neck supplied me with a concoction of drugs and fluids, while the ventilator pumped air into my lungs, the rhythmic beeping giving comfort to the staff that I was still alive.

I have little recollection of my first few days, and in my drugged haze I apparently told Mum, 'I want to die!'

'No, we love you and we are taking you home with us,' she said. I don't recall saying it, but I guess the news of my situation left little hope in my mind at the time, although I don't remember feeling that way.

In my brief moments of wakefulness, the drugs did little to dull the pain in my nose caused by the garden-hose-sized tube from the ventilator stretching my poor nostril to the point of splitting as it reached down into my lungs. The worst feeling was in my mouth: it was so dry my tongue stuck to the roof and the sides, with nothing to swallow. I begged the nurse for a drink, which was out of the question: 'No food or drink allowed for you, David,' she said. Out of pity and probably sick of me asking, she stuck what felt like a large swab or big cotton-wool bud into my mouth. Being ventilated meant I couldn't taste or smell anything but I could sense a cool, sweet, lemon flavour, and I sucked so hard to get the thirst-quenching nectar out of it. It had only a fraction of moisture but, feeling so desperate for fluid, it was like sucking on a juicy Zooper Dooper icy-pole.

My parents came in each day, my sisters periodically, like a tag team. Kathryn is the eldest, six years older than me, and was then a nurse at the Alfred Hospital. Next came Marg, who was living in Western Australia. She and her partner, John, had set out to travel around Australia, then settled with jobs in Port Hedland where they had been for the last few years. EJ was studying computer science at university (that is, when she wasn't travelling overseas). Then there was me; and finally Madeleine, born two years after me, doing VCE in high school at the time of my accident.

My sisters are very independent people, with strong views and ideas on everything. They say what they think, which invariably leads to what you might call 'robust' discussions. Our house was never quiet. Discussions were loud, a necessity to get your point across; the loudest usually won. My parents would just sit back and let it happen. What else could they do with five kids barking like hyenas at each other?

Battles were fought over many things, as siblings do, but with only one TV in the house, the most common feuds erupted over our favourite TV shows and what we would watch. However, my parents worked out an ingenious plan. Each kid could have one night per week of being in charge of the TV. But the catch was, you had to do the dishes and clean up on that night. Brilliant: no dishes, no TV! It worked a treat, turning the fights into diplomacy that would rival the best United Nations negotiations.

Although it may have sounded like WWIII, when the arguments were over, they were forgotten and no grudges were ever held. My family was always loving and supportive, they were always there when needed, and I needed them now more than ever.

Life at home had changed completely. My family was devastated, numb with grief. Dad said, 'It was like being in a dream that you had no control over, totally surreal,' as they grappled with the dribs and drabs of information from the doctors and nursing staff, trying to make sense of it. Everyone was significantly affected: Madeleine and EJ were terribly upset, trying to deal with the situation and do their studies, while Kathryn had recently been accepted by Qantas as a flight attendant with training in Sydney, but was considering quitting to look after me. Mum told her I would be upset if she missed the opportunity because of me and advised her to go up there. I'm glad she did. Marg in Port Hedland found it doubly hard being so far away. At the same time, there wasn't much she could do, so it was decided she would come home when I moved into rehabilitation, if I made it that far. My family was told to keep busy, so everyone continued with their lives as best they could as the most effective way to deal with their trauma. Dad went back to work a couple of days later and Mum had two weeks off from teaching at a high school, visiting me each day.

No one understood what quadriplegia meant or what I would or wouldn't eventually be able to do—and with little understanding of what the future would be, Mum's immediate reaction was to quit work and look after me for the rest of my life.

The hospital staff were exceptional in their support of my family, and Dr Brown, the head of the spinal department, was helpfully blunt: 'If you're depressed, David will be depressed. If you are positive, David will be positive,' he said. This helped them deal with the situation, and it was certainly better for me. It was at that point that my family decided they would do whatever it took to help me live as full a life as was possible.

Friends came to the hospital and waited in the visitors' room, but I was too sick to see anyone but my family. Mum, Dad, Kathryn, EJ and Madeleine came in throughout the day and read *The Secret Diary of Adrian Mole* to me. As I drifted to sleep, they would stop and when I awoke, resume reading. I loved being read to, hearing about this kid who had a strange view of the world, looking at the funny side of his everyday life.

The book gave me some escape, taking my mind off my 'imprisonment'—the beeping, the tubes, the pains in my nose, arms and shoulders—the nightmare I was in. I quietly laughed at Adrian Mole's embarrassing and unique perspectives on life. These reminded me of some of my embarrassing moments, such as the time my dad replaced the blue seat on my Dragster bicycle with a bright pink one with sparkles— 'It was on sale,' he said. With a fear of complete and utter embarrassment from which my reputation would never recover, I didn't ride my bike to primary school for a long time after that.

Day or night, time was irrelevant to me and each day blurred into the next. Four days after being admitted to the Austin Hospital I had my twentieth birthday, 14 July 1988. One of the nurses suggested a party was in order (not that I would be attending), as it would be a good way to tell my friends and neighbours about my situation and how they could best help. Mum and Dad arranged drinks and food, and they all reminisced and cried in the waiting room of the ICU as they learnt about my disability. Only my family was allowed to come in and see me, so Mum brought in a cake with white icing and blue writing, and held up my present: a cream-coloured jumper with a grey pattern that sort of looked like an Aztec design. Given my situation, it was probably the most practical gift they could get me as no one had any idea what I would be like when, or if, I made it out of hospital. I still needed clothes, no matter what my condition would be.

I certainly wasn't feeling in the party mood. With my lung capacity now reduced to 50 percent, the bronchitis I had before the accident, made worse by smoking, turned into a very solid dose of pneumonia. The infection built up in my lungs, clogging them like a sponge soaked in used motor oil.

But I did get some good news: the tube down my nose would be removed and replaced with a tracheostomy. With a 'trachy,' a hole would be cut in my neck and a tube inserted into the windpipe to enable the air to bypass the mouth—which meant I couldn't talk. I could only mouth words, and people had to read my lips. Some of the nurses were quite good and my family got the hang of it, but some people just couldn't grasp the skill. After saying something five times, I usually gave up.

Also, with a trachy I still couldn't smell or taste food, which made everything very bland. Food became a matter of texture for me. This probably wasn't a bad thing as the food in hospitals is usually pretty ordinary anyway.

The nurses and doctors had sold this trachy idea to me as a positive development: 'No more sore nose!' I was told. Fantastic! Just a hole cut into my throat and whack in a bit of plastic tube to connect the ventilator. Great! Little did I know what their true intentions were. Chest physio—whatever that was.

As I soon learned, chest physio was used to inflate the lungs to help loosen the greeny-yellow, slimy, pussy phlegm build-up in my lungs. 'It's just like taking a big deep breath,' they said. Sounds harmless, doesn't it?

In reality, often a trainee physio who'd done little chest physio on a real person would come in, attach a black bag the size of bagpipes to my newly installed tracheostomy, then squeeze and inflate my lungs repeatedly. The pressure would build to the point where I thought my chest would explode and I would fly around the room like a balloon. It was bloody painful. With all the phlegmy gunk building up around the inside of my trachy from the repeated inflations, I'd gurgle away like a clogged sink.

The suction device would then be produced. A long, thin plastic tube was fed down through my trachy to suck out the contents of my lungs into a bottle behind my head on the wall. This was usually a relief unless they went too far and hit the inside of the windpipe, producing a pain akin to having your eyes burnt out. I never realised there are sensory nerves inside some of our organs, in particular the windpipe. Then again, our bodies weren't designed to have holes punched through to our insides and have tubes stuck in while awake either.

One inflation, two inflations, three inflations, four inflations, then suck gunk out! This was done four times in a session, every six hours. At times I had tears streaming down my face, begging them to stop from the pain.

I soon realised that to avoid the pain, I needed to give some guidance to the newbies and train them up. By getting the students to read my lips, and to watch the expressions on my face—whether the tears or lack thereof reflecting my comfort level—I managed to eventually train and get most of the young physios quite proficient.

Going to the toilet had never entered my mind; I was too preoccupied with trying to stop becoming unconscious, without much success so far. I hadn't eaten or drunk anything for a number of days since the night of my accident, so what was left in my body was still happily sitting there as some of my bodily functions had come to a halt.

The radio crackled to life, signalling 6 a.m. with the song 'Perfect' by Fairground Attraction, which was played at around the same time most days. This was the only way I could roughly judge what time it was. The orderlies or 'turners,' as they were called—mainly because they turned the patients over periodically to avoid pressure sores from lying in one position for too long—turned me onto my left side. This was a coordinated procedure requiring four people to turn my body and head (with the head tongs and weights attached) at exactly the same time from back to side. Any misaligned moves could cause more damage to my fragile spinal cord and vertebrae. Although rare, a slight twisting of the head tongs produced a sensation of a skewer being thrust through my temples.

Tania, the nurse looking after me this particular morning, started doing something behind me. I mouthed to her, 'What are you doing?'

'I'm putting in a suppository. You're going to the toilet today,' she said with a little excitement in her voice.

Really? But how? was the question in my mind. I didn't feel like going. I was in bed and I couldn't move.

Half an hour or so later Tania came back. I knew she was up to something as I could hear the rustling of plastic and paper. I couldn't feel anything apart from a mildly uncomfortable pain in my shoulder that had turned into a nagging, hurry-the-fuck-up ache. To get her attention I did my Skippy impersonation (Skippy is a kangaroo from a '60s Australian TV show that communicated by sounding 'click, click, click'). 'What are you doing?' I mouthed.

'I'm cleaning you up. You're coming out like soft-serve!' she said. An image of brown soft-serve ice cream swirling onto a cone filled my mind.

I couldn't smell anything due to my trachy, which was a plus, nor could I feel anything. I hadn't comprehended the state my body was in. Apart from my aching shoulder, my whole body was numb;

it seemed detached from me like the rest of the world.

Tania talked to me while she cleaned up the toxic biowaste, trying to make me feel at ease, but I couldn't help feeling degraded. I was a helpless baby being cleaned up. I lay there, my mind numb to what was happening, trying to make sense of what this meant for me. But this was only the start.

I regained a little more movement as the swelling of my spinal cord reduced. The doctors told my parents that after six weeks, whatever movement I had by that stage was pretty much going to be it. Of course, some further movement can come back or get stronger some months later—although the change is less significant.

The second week in ICU, Dr Brown did his rounds. It was time to see what movement remained. Doctors usually give you the worst-case scenario: I guess in their view it's better to have low expectations, and if it turns out better, it's a bonus.

I couldn't see what was going on. Dr Brown said, 'Can you feel this?' as he pricked my leg.

'No,' I mouthed.

As he worked down lower and lower towards my foot, I still had no sensation. He lifted a right leg up into my view. *Oh, that's mine*, I thought. It was so weird; it didn't feel as though it belonged to me, it seemed totally detached.

'Can you move your toes?' he asked. I tried with all my might, but nothing moved. Not even a flicker. My legs, my whole body below my armpits, was dead.

Breaking the fifth vertebrae meant that if I had movement to this level only, I would have very limited arm function, and no hand function at all. I would be very restricted in what I could do.

Dr Brown inspected my hands. 'Can you move your fingers?' he said. I tried, but nothing. 'David, try lifting your right wrist up.'

I tried again with all my might; it moved up weakly. Dr Brown and Christine, the occupational therapist attending, seemed quite pleased. It was weak but there was some movement. Checking my left wrist, I had a little more mobility than the right.

I didn't understand this at the time, but having even a little wrist extension (when my palm is facing down, having the ability to raise the back of my hand towards the back of my forearm) meant that I had some additional movement beyond my level of injury—that is, to the sixth vertebrae. This little bit of movement would make a big difference to my life in terms of what I would be able to do.

4
13 EAST

After two weeks in ICU, and feeling much better, I was moved to Ward 13 East for my remaining one-and-a-half-month stay in bed. I had come off the ventilator, but still had the trachy to deal with my chest infection, though this had reduced significantly. Chest physio four times a day was still my torture routine.

The nurses did the feeding rounds, three times a day dispensing food from a huge enclosed rattling stainless-steel trolley. I still couldn't smell or taste food with the trachy, and sucking tasteless, lukewarm, watery soup through a straw didn't give me much to look forward to. One advantage of having a trachy was that I couldn't choke, so eating while lying on my back wasn't a problem. Most of the nurses were pretty good at feeding, but there were the occasional ones who needed to keep their minds on the job. A sharp 'click, click, click,' of my Skippy speak got them back on the task of shovelling the food in.

Not long after my transfer to 13 East I got a collapsed lung. A young doctor who reminded me of Doogie Howser (a medical-comedy show from the early '90s, the main character being a teenaged doctor) gave me a rundown on my situation and what they planned to do about it. Basically, one of my lungs wasn't working properly, being full of pussy mucus that had to be removed. So much for all my chest physio: they had sucked at least my body weight of crap out of me, and I didn't think there would be anything left.

I should have got the idea when Virginia the nurse said, 'David, would you like some pethidine, it might be a little uncomfortable?'

'No thanks!' *I can handle a little uncomfortable,* I thought.

I didn't know what I was in for but Annette, a lovely young blonde nurse with a huge smile and a lot of makeup, did. She put her hand in mine, anticipating what I was about to experience as I briefly glimpsed out of the corner of my eye something long heading towards my throat.

'OK, I'm entering the trachy now,' said Doogie.

BANG! STAB! The tube hit the inside walls of my windpipe as it went down, like fish-hooks being dragged into my lungs. *Faaaarck!* I screamed inside my head as the tube went deeper, the pain intensifying as if a blowtorch was being waved over the walls of my insides.

As warm tears streamed down past my temples, I looked up at Annette; she had tears in her eyes as she watched me mouth the words to the doctor, 'Stop, Stop!'

Fuck, I really wish I had the pethidine now! I thought.

'It will be over soon, Dave,' said Annette, squeezing my hand a little tighter.

The seconds dragged on as though they were minutes. 'We're almost done,' Doogie said calmly as he pushed the tube in deeper. *Bang,* another burst of pain as the blowtorch in my lungs turned into a flamethrower, my chest feeling as though it was about to explode.

'That's it, well done,' Doogie said. I gasped as the tube was pulled from my throat; the relief was as quick as the pain was inflicted.

I lay there trying to recover and comprehend what had just happened as Annette wiped the tears from my eyes.

I put in extra effort with my chest physio after that; there was no way in the world I was going to have another bronchoscopy. They'd have to knock me out first.

With little to do except wait for the hours to slowly drift by, my view changed like the rising and setting sun, being turned from back to side every four hours. When on my back, the range of vision was straight up, at the ceiling. On my side, for pressure relief, I faced either a blue curtain on my right which separated my area from the patient next to me, or the cupboards on my left side. Taped to the grey door of the cupboard was a picture of me at Smiths Beach, Phillip Island, just after a surf. It looked like a hot day, sand dunes in the background, the wetsuit pulled down to my waist showing off my partially hairy and muscled chest, T-shirt-tanned guns, and the classic '80s big hair with a full-on mullet. I tried to draw out every detail in the picture to relive the freedom I'd experienced on that day with my mate Dave and girlfriend Tanya. I wished so much that I was there again.

My world had now become the holes and stains on the ceiling tiles above my head and the faces that peered over me throughout the day. Old brown sticky-tape marks were scattered across the ceiling tiles from past patients whose pictures of family, friends, drawings from their kids or something special kept them going while they lay in bed day after day, not knowing what their future would be. I wondered who those people were. How had they ended up here? Were they like me; did they feel the same?

The nurses adjusted the mirrors above my head so I could see images at the foot of my bed. It gave me another view that would at least change occasionally when someone walked by.

I could hear the other patients and I knew who they were by their voices, but I never saw their faces. I imagined what the room looked like and painted portraits of each person's face in my mind from the sound of their voice. Bill, next to me at my three o'clock, sounded like he was from the country. I imagined he had a skinny, tanned and weathered face from years of being outside, with grey stubble and sharp grey eyes. Graham at my six o'clock had a deep voice. He had a pale, round, fat face, a big nose with broken red capillaries like a road atlas, sunken eyes and a receding hairline. Stephan at my five o'clock was silent like me. He was a seventeen-year-old from a Greek family, who came in the same time as me following a car accident. He was in the navy and one Saturday night when out with mates, the driver lost control of the car, rolled it, and Stephan snapped his neck. We were considered a pair as we both broke the same vertebrae and had the same level of function, C5 incomplete, C6 complete. I had imagined Stephan to look like a skinny Greek kid, with olive skin and big hair.

My day was broken up into small segments of time. Three times a day I was fed, the nurses did their observations every couple of hours, the physio came four times a day to give me chest physio and stretch my legs and arms to maintain flexibility. The occupational therapist dropped by daily to stretch my hands and get me to exercise my wrists by lifting them up and down with a light weight strapped on. Each bit of strength I could build up would be invaluable to my rehab and independence. At least their visits gave me breaks from the monotony: sleeping or staring at the ceiling all day.

Mum and Dad came in each afternoon, telling me about their day, what my sisters were up to and passing on messages from other people. It seemed so removed from my little world and my daily routine. As they talked about each person, my memories flashed back to what I knew before the accident. The pictures in my mind were so clear, as if it was yesterday: EJ studying on the floor at home with her books and papers spread out in a coordinated mess, Madeleine at school and going out in her black gothic attire, Mum and Dad going to work and then doing the usual stuff around home, with Dad out in the garden. How quickly my life had changed from normality to where I was now. It just didn't seem real. I wasn't worried, because I was oblivious to what was in store for me. I had no idea how long or how hard I would have to struggle just to relearn some of the most basic daily living tasks we all take for granted, let alone get my life back to some semblance of what I once had.

The rest of the time I lay there with nothing to do. The TV above my head was on an adjustable arm enabling it to be moved to the best viewing angle above my head, but the shows during the day, like the soapie *The Bold and the Beautiful*, were not ones I could get into, no matter how desperate I was. I began to watch late into the night when some better viewing was on, and sleep throughout the day. Thankfully the TVs had a video link to the rooms, enabling the patients to bring in a video and watch it in bed. I put in my order and Mum brought in the latest releases, each giving me an opportunity to escape from my world for a couple of hours. *Running Man* with Arnold Schwarzenegger was a favourite, and everyone in the ward watched it.

Having my voice taken away, although temporarily, made me realise how important it was. Not being able to communicate was so isolating. The nurses and orderlies were well practised with lip-reading so I could have a normal conversation with them most of the time, and my family got the hang of it eventually. But it was hard initially, and worse when a new person dropped by. Having to repeat myself time and time again to make someone understand what I was trying to say was very tiring and frustrating.

'Hi Dave, how are you?'

'Good. How are you?' I'd mouth with no sound.

'You're good?'

'Yes,' I'd mouth.

'Click, click, click,' I'd sound to get their attention.

'Can you pass me a cup of water with the straw,' I'd mouth.

'Say that again?'

'Water, can you give me some water,' I'd mouth again.

'Water?' they'd say louder, as if I was starting to go a little deaf.

'Yes.'

'Oh, OK, from the tap?'

'No, the jug,' I'd mouth.

'From where?' Leaning closer in the hope that some faint word might come out.

'Jug, jug!' I'd mouth.

'The jug?'

'Yes!'

'This?'

'Yes!'

'Do I use this cup?'

'Yes.'

'Need a straw!' I'd mouth.

'What was that?'

'Need straw.'

'Store?'

'Straw, straw, straw!!' I'd mouth in frustration.

With blank expressions, they'd stop to imitate my mouth movements and think about what I could be asking.

'Store, Shtore, strore, straw,' their faces lighting up in hope.

'Straw?'

'Yes!' I let out a big sigh, rolling my eyes.

'This one?'

'Yes!'

Depending on who it was, I'd weigh up how much effort was required before asking for something or entering into a conversation.

My inability to communicate made my situation even more confronting for visitors. I could see the shock and anguish on their faces as they took in my withering body, covered only by a sheet from my waist down, head tongs screwed into my skull attached to a rope pulling my neck straight. And on top of it all, having to read my lips for a conversation.

A month or so after the accident, the day finally came when I was to have my trachy blocked off, then hopefully removed a few days later.

I couldn't wait. I would be able to breathe through my mouth again, relieved of the frustration of visitors having to read my lips, and I would finally be able to taste food.

My anticipation and excitement felt akin to what Neil Armstrong must have experienced when he took the first step on the moon and uttered the famous words, 'A small step for man, a giant leap for mankind.' It was a big step for me. I would be a step closer to making the leap to recovery and back into my life.

The nurse put the cap over the trachy tube to block it off. *Woosh!* A blast of cold air streamed over my tongue, around the inside of my mouth, down my throat and into my lungs. The frigid, cooling sensation seemed so foreign. Breathing out again, I rediscovered the forgotten sensation of warmth as I exhaled.

My first words that I had longed to pass my lips over the last month came out as a forced, croaky declaration of, 'God, my mouth tastes terrible!' I could now imagine what the inside of a sewer pipe must taste like.

The first sip of the bland, watery, lukewarm tomato soup through a straw was tantalising as my taste buds went into overdrive at the burst of sweet tomatoey flavour; it was the most wonderful thing I had ever tasted.

Mum had anticipated my longing for one of my favourite meals that I had been dreaming of for weeks: fish and chips. Lying on my back, being fed chips and fried dim-sims, making my habitual 'click, click, click' to signal the insertion of the next chip into my mouth, was fantastic. But God help the person feeding me who got distracted talking: he or she got a severe lashing of 'click, click, click, click, click, click' until a chip plugged the hole.

There were some drawbacks though, in particular, regaining my sense of smell. Four people in the same room having their bowels opened on the same morning stunk worse than the Werribee sewerage farm. With my nose sensors heightened, the smell hung so thick in the air I could almost taste it.

'Nurse, is there a fan?' I pleaded.

'No, breathe through your mouth!' she said.

Having my voice again was a turning point; I was a step closer to regaining Me. Being able to speak with my family transformed the visits, as it did with my friends. People could see that I was the same person, joking, being a smart-arse and flirting with the nurses. Even though I was stuck in bed, I was still me.

It was great to have many of my friends come in, to see their familiar faces and hear about what they were up to. I envied them, their lives continuing as I lay in my isolated world. I wished I was out there with them.

The confronting sight of me was still a challenge for some. Some of my mates, mostly the male ones, would joke around saying, 'When you get out, Jacka, we'll go out like old times. You'll be right, mate!' What do you say to someone who looks completely stuffed? This was just them wrestling with their discomfort, trying to deal with the situation as best as they could.

Pete, my best mate since primary school who was at Macca's on the night of my accident, had a tough time following my accident. The visits to the hospital wouldn't have made it any easier. It's always emotionally challenging when anyone close to us is injured. I've often wondered if there was an element of guilt involved. But as far as I'm concerned, it was no one's fault but my own. I made the decision to ride the bike that night; it was my responsibility alone, and I paid the price of that decision.

My female friends seemed to be more comfortable seeing me, more accepting of my state. I guess it came from being more in touch with their feelings, willing to express themselves. I had more female friends than male ones, maybe due to growing up with four sisters. In any case, I am comfortable around those of the opposite sex. I had some very close female friends who were a great support. Tanya came in often; we had broken up a few months before the accident but had still hung out a lot together. There were also my friends Becky and Suzie, sisters I met through our parents; then Robyn, who lived just around the corner from me. A few of us would hang out at her place in the evenings, talking, smoking and drinking coffee and tea.

My friends dealt with my situation as best they could and in their own ways, with many giving me encouragement, support and friendship. With some, like Tanya, I saw a deeper side of love, kindness and a willingness to support me in whatever way was necessary. This shone through even though Tanya's own life was in turmoil at the time, with her parents divorcing and their family dog being put down. I was and remain truly grateful for her friendship.

I was aware that my friendship dynamics had shifted, which was understandable given my situation, but I didn't want anything to change. I was the same person, and I hung on to the sliver of hope that it would all go back to normal when I got home.

Visits from my family and friends only filled in a small portion of the day: there were few distractions to break the boredom throughout the long days and nights. Starved of anything else to quell the tedium, the interruptions of the nurses doing their observation rounds, feeding, turning, toileting, giving me a drink or the daily wash, all tended to break the monotony. Staff were mostly young, unquestionably caring and friendly, and always up for a chat. Being stuck in one place for so long, it is inevitable that you develop a rapport or a connection with some, where the brief moments of conversation grow into more personal bedside relationships. I got glimpses into their personal lives: their families, boyfriends, or what they did on their days off. I got to know a couple of the nurses well, and some the friendships went beyond the walls of the hospital.

In 13 East, Tina, an attractive, dark-haired Italian nurse of twenty-five (a mature woman, given my age of twenty) worked nights, and apart from letting me into her personal world outside of the hospital, talking about her family and her life, we also chatted about food—one of the simple pleasures I was missing from having to survive on hospital food.

'So, Tein, you say you can cook?'

'Of course, I'm Italian.'

'That doesn't mean you can cook.'

'Yes it does, it's in our genes.'

'Well, yes, you do have good jeans,' I said cheekily.

She gave a chuckle and smiled.

'I'm sure your mum is a good cook, but that doesn't mean you are,' I said with a grin.

'Well, you don't have to believe me, but I'm pretty good. Mum has some special family recipes that I know how to do.'

'Really? So what are these recipes?'

'They're secret.'

'Aww… you can't tell me they're secret. Come on, what are they?'

'Nup!'

'I bet one is spaghetti bolognese? I loooooove a good spag bol!'

'Mum said Dad only married her for her spaghetti!'

'Really?'

'Yup.'

'What makes it so good?'

'I can't tell you that, it's a secret!'

'Aww… You're just saying that.'

'No really, Mum would kill me!'

'Tein, spag bol is one of my favourites.'

'Well, I'm making some this week. If you're lucky, I might bring some in for you to try!'

'Ha ha, don't tease me, Tein.'

Good to her word, Tina brought me some of her secret recipe spaghetti bolognese. After eating hospital food for so long, the complexity of textures and flavours—garlic, herbs, carrots, beef mince, fat and red wine—blew my senses. I was in heaven.

'Will you marry me?' I asked with a saucy grin.

'Ha ha! I told you it was good.'

The months in bed allowed for a lot of thinking time, particularly about what my life would be like in the future. Some nights I couldn't sleep and lay awake thinking, an ever-present nagging feeling of being adrift in an expansive ocean. What I really wanted to know was: what would I be able to do? 'You should be able to push a wheelchair along flat ground,' was the best I got from a doctor.

I knew I couldn't move anything from my armpits down; my arm movements were uncoordinated, and I couldn't move them in every direction due to the loss of function. I understood what the doctors had told me about my level of function: I wouldn't walk, and it was unlikely I would gain any more movement. But how that translated into what I would or wouldn't be able to do was a concept I couldn't fully grasp until I experienced it. It's no different from trying to imagine what chocolate tastes like if you have never tried it. Someone can tell you what it's like, but you will never know the taste and texture until you have experienced it yourself. At the time, the staff were doing every single thing for me, so until I got out of bed, I wouldn't understand the extent of my injury and its impact on my life. As I lay there, fantasising about getting out of hospital, the image of myself in my mind was of what I looked like before my accident: an able-bodied twenty-year-old, fit, strong, well-built, but just sitting in a wheelchair.

As Christine, my occupational therapist (OT), did the daily stretches of my hands and fingers, I said to her, 'You know, when I get up, I'm going to push up the hill out there.'

She peered at me sideways, raising her eyebrows with a tight-lipped half smile.

'Burgundy Street? That's pretty steep,' she said, looking away. I wasn't deterred. At that point, I was still in my pre-accident way of thinking. As far as I was concerned, I was still six-foot-three and bullet-proof, and I could do anything physically.

The inactive weeks were taking their toll on my body; the muscles that still functioned were shrivelling away like dried jerky from not being used. But I was feeling pretty good apart from the broken neck. I felt motivated and wanted to get arm weights so I could at least work them a little as I lay in bed for the remaining few weeks. After discussions with the doctors to ensure that my neck wouldn't be damaged further by using weights, the physio hooked up some light springs to the foot of the bed and tied a bandage from the spring to my wrist on each arm.

Twice a day the physio hooked me up so I could do my workout—I slowly built up to four sets of ten reps, pushing myself to do more. Whether it made much difference to my mobility once I got up, I don't know, but it was more of a psychological benefit that gave me a goal to aim for, something positive to do while lying in bed for so long.

'When we unscrew the bolts on the head tongs, it will initially feel like they are being tightened,' the nurse said, just as I heard the spanner clanging against the bolt on the side of my head. The cracking and grinding as the bolt rotated in my skull echoed like a vast canyon in my head, my face contorting with the quick sharp pain of a meat skewer being twisted through the side of my head; then suddenly, relief.

The day had come, and I was going to be mobilised after two months of lying in bed. I couldn't wait. I had been thinking about this day for so long, but it always seemed so far away. Now it was about to happen, and I would be able to get on with my life.

As each little milestone was crossed, it was celebrated. As I was being turned onto my side one night, the orderly said to Sally, the nurse, 'He's wet, the sheets need to be changed.' Sally squealed with delight. 'You're autoing,' she said, then ran off to get the duty nurse to share the good news. When a person with quadriplegia 'autos,' it means the bladder is starting to contract automatically, squeezing out urine, in turn emptying the bladder. This was good news for me, as it most likely meant that I would use condom drainage—a special condom with an adhesive that attaches to my penis, which is then connected to a tube attached to a leg-bag into which the urine drains. If all went to plan, I would pee automatically into the leg-bag, not requiring the need to self-catheterise: a process where a thin tube is shoved up my 'Johnson' into the bladder to drain it every four hours. The other option at the time was to have an indwelling catheter wherein a rubber hose is permanently stuck up your 'old fella' to drain the bladder—not a very pleasant method.

I was very glad to be 'autoing,' another milestone down, but I didn't quite share Sally's level of enthusiasm.

After lying horizontal for so long, my body wasn't used to sitting upright. In addition to my quadriplegia, I now had lower blood pressure. It was going to be a slow process to begin sitting up and finally get into the wheelchair.

Stephan; the Greek kid with a broken neck opposite, and I were to be mobilised at the same time. First, we had to prove that the muscles in our necks were strong enough to hold our heads up sufficiently. The orderlies turned us onto our stomachs, and with a soft block under our foreheads to stop our faces from being squashed and us potentially suffocating, we had to lift our heads up off the block for thirty seconds before we could go on to the next step.

Not a problem, I thought. I was always stronger than everybody else, and I was determined not to be beaten and to achieve the thirty seconds.

'Time starts now,' Jenny the nurse said. I lifted my head. *God, it weighs a tonne, I don't remember it being this heavy*, I thought.

As the seconds slowly ticked by, Stephan dropped his head in defeat. My head was getting heavier, but I would not give up. The muscles in my neck burned, then, just as I thought I couldn't go any further, Jenny called, 'Thirty seconds.

'Well done, David,' she said.

'Thank Christ,' I said, panting with exhaustion.

With my neck muscles so weak, I was fitted with a neck collar to hold my head in place and help support it for the first two months while my neck stabilised.

The next phase was to sit me up slowly in bed. On the first day the bed's backrest was raised twenty degrees, three times a day, followed by forty degrees on day two, then around sixty degrees on day three.

Each time I was sat up, my world changed a little more. I could see more of the room, which didn't fit the image in my mind. It was smaller, and seeing people from upright positions was a novelty compared to them leaning over me or through the mirrors.

On day three of my mobilisation as I was raised to the highest position, which felt like I was bolt upright although it was only sixty degrees, I had the most peculiar sensation. I could see my legs out in front of me covered with white pressure stockings to prevent swelling. But they didn't feel like my legs—they seemed completely detached. Also, the pressure on my bum made me feel as though I was standing up with my legs going down through the bed to the floor.

Day four, 'M-Day,' I was finally 'mobilised' and began the first stage of my wheelchair-bound existence: the recliner wheelchair. It looked more like a Jason Recliner sofa chair on wheels, with the high back and headrest angled back and the legs raised to put my body in a reclined, almost flat position so I wouldn't pass out.

My world had changed again, expanding a little more to the boundaries of the ward. It was strange seeing everyone from my new vantage point: they all looked so different, yet the same. I had to giggle when I saw Stephan: he looked nothing like the Greek kid I had imagined. He had orange hair, a pale complexion and freckles, but he did have the big '80s hair. I felt more comfortable and I suppose happier that my family and friends could now see some progress towards me getting better.

For the next couple of days, I spent short periods in the wheelchair to let my body adjust to the more vertical position and allow the skin on my bum to build up tolerance to being sat on. Initially, every fifteen minutes the nurses leant me over in the Jason Recliner to take pressure off my bum, letting the blood circulate to avoid pressure sores. Virginia and Sally, my nurses, fussed over me, feeding me, doing everything for me, and making sure everything was OK. In my cocoon, my room, my world, I was comfortable and safe.

It was only days until I was to be transferred to the rehabilitation ward when a bed became available. Two months since my rebirth into my Second Life, my world would change again.

5

PALE-BLUE WALL

The Get Well, We Are Thinking of You, Happy Birthday cards and photos were taken down from the wall above the bed and cupboards, packed away with my meagre belongings into large, reinforced paper bags, ready for transport to Ward 17, the rehabilitation ward.

Saying my goodbyes to the nurses and staff, I felt a little sad that I was leaving these wonderful people, some of whom had shared with me aspects of their personal lives from the bedside and nursed me back to health—apart from the stuffed spine which could not be repaired.

But mixed with the sadness was the excitement, the anticipation of taking another step away from the night of my accident and the incapacitation of the bed towards the future—whatever that would be.

With my belongings up at Ward 17, Sally jumped on the back of my recliner wheelchair, just tall enough to peer over the headrest to see where we were going. Poking her head from side to side as she pushed the lumbering wheelchair to avoid collecting any unsuspecting bystanders, we headed off down the corridor towards my future.

As the squeak of Sally's rubber-soled shoes on the vinyl floor faded behind me, the deafening silence of my new room strangled me like a straitjacket, broken only by faint intermittent noises from other patients who seemed so far away.

I stared at the pale-blue wall in front of me, unable to move my head, held tight by the neck brace, propped on top of the paralysed body below me. I reached down with my weak, uncoordinated, spindly arms and fumbled as I tried to put my hands on the wheels in a vain attempt to move the huge steel recliner wheelchair. The wonderful image I had craftily painted in my mind of myself as an invincible bloke was suddenly shattered.

My whole life up to this moment had been about what I could do physically: it was my whole identity. Everything I did and enjoyed in my life—my job, surfing, snow-skiing, being outside, knocking around with mates—was about being fully able, being tougher, stronger, more physically capable than most other people. I was now finished. The sudden, crushing realisation that all I had imagined or hoped for was a fantasy: I felt as if my life was over.

My body, once my capsule for freedom, was now my prison. The pale-blue wall loomed nearer, closing in around me. All my hopes and dreams, big and small—starting a building business, travelling the world, finding someone to share my life with, following my boyhood dream of learning to fly—evaporated like a drop of water on a red-hot skillet, with the realisation that I was completely fucked.

Christine, the OT, was right: I wasn't going to be pushing up that hill. Even the thought of pushing a wheelchair on flat ground seemed impossible.

As the tears poured down my face, a nurse came in. Obviously experienced with blubbering patients, she gave me a few comforting words, and then called 13 East.

Within minutes Sally was back up. 'Let's get out of here, Dave,' she whispered in my ear from behind, and rushed me outside to the café area.

I wasn't prepared for the shock of my new reality. During my bedridden two months, I'd pictured myself in a wheelchair and, although unable to walk, I imagined strong arms and a cool look with my sunglasses. I now realised this was a distorted fantasy.

Sally parked me next to the bench, sat down beside me and put her warm hand on mine. 'You OK?'

With watering eyes, I struggled to get my words out. 'S-s-sorry Sal, I'm not sure what happened there.'

'It was all a bit much, ay?' she said.

I nodded. 'I think it was just a bit of a shock,' I said.

'You know, it's gonna be OK. It just takes a bit of time.'

I nodded again.

'Just don't forget about us, will you. And make sure you come for a visit,' she said with a warm smile.

'How could I forget about you, Sal? Oh yeah, you still owe me that curry!'

Now that I was a little more in control, Sally took me back up to face the next stage of my life with quadriplegia.

Mum and Dad had arrived and were waiting in my room. My side was still bare of my possessions, so the nurse quickly unpacked my cards to try and make it a little more welcoming.

In this ward, if you needed something like a TV to watch in bed at night, a family member had to bring it in for you. It was like going from the Hilton Hotel into housing commission.

The new routine had me in bed by 7 p.m., making it a very long night. Fortunately, Dad managed to persuade the charge nurse to allow the big TV from the lounge to be wheeled in to at least provide me with some distraction to pass the time on my first night.

As I lay on my side, with a pillow wedged behind my back to stop me rolling over, the flickering light of the TV flashed on the walls. But I couldn't watch it. I felt numb. I wished I wasn't there.

My memories and dreams were of another life, when I was me, when I was whole. I wondered what my future would be. I had always known where I was going, I'd always had a plan, but now my road map was blank. I couldn't see a future.

6

FIRST DAY

Following a broken night's sleep of being turned every four hours and having my bladder drained by catheter to see how much urine was in it, I was abruptly awoken at 7 a.m. to the high-pitched screech of 'Cuppa teeeeeah, cuppa teeeeeah!' This was the calling cry of a friendly old Italian tea lady, pushing her clanging and rumbling trolley laden with a full hot-water urn, tea, coffee, plastic cups and biscuits, ready to serve to the patients on the ward.

The building was buzzing with orderlies and nurses getting those patients up who needed either full or partial help. Being the newbie, I was left till last when all the other patients were up and out to breakfast.

My rehabilitation started that day; however, I use the word 'rehabilitation' loosely. The purpose of the next six months was to provide me with some basic skills and an understanding of my disability so I could at least function when I eventually went home. Every day for the next few months would be an overwhelming series of new experiences mixed with frustration and boredom.

That morning was my first proper shower for over two months, and I couldn't wait. My hair was starting to feel a little Jamaicany, and the thought of sitting under the warm running water caressing every inch of my body—at least the bits I could feel—was so enticing.

The orderlies strapped an abdominal binder (a tight elastic belt) around my stomach to help me breathe and not pass out when I sat up, then lifted me onto a commode wheelchair. The nurse wheeled me into the cubicle, a splash here, a splash there, a good scrub with the face-washer and soap, another splash here and there to hose off the soap, a semi-vigorous dry off, except for my head which had to be held very still in my neck brace as it was still unstable, and that was it. With so many patients to get up, there was very little time in the mornings; it was a rush to get everyone off and ready for the day. I was so disappointed. I'd have to wait a long time before I would be able to luxuriate under the running water of a shower.

Before I came to rehab, my parents were given strict instructions on what the new 'uniform' would be for their son once he was mobilised. And last night after my little mental readjustment, Mum presented me with a surprise.

'David, I bought you some new clothes.'

Having your mum buy you new clothes without your approval is a little scary.

'What new clothes?' I asked.

'Jackie the nurse said you will need some loose-fitting clothes, so I got you these,' she said, pulling out three pairs of blue tracksuit pants with an orange fluorescent stripe down the sides. 'What do you think?'

'Tracksuits? I don't wear tracksuits!'

'The nurse said you will need tracksuit pants, so I'm doing what they say.'

'They look big!'

'They're your size, David, I measured your jeans.'

'They still look big!'

'Try them on tomorrow, and if they are too big I will return them. You need something, so these will have to do for now.'

'Couldn't you get Adidas ones?'

'Adeedas?'

'Its Ad-di-das, Mum!'

'I think with Adidas you had to buy the whole tracksuit. I didn't think you would like that.'

'That's OK. The pants will be fine.'

'But I got you some Adeedas shoes. You've had these before,' she said as she pulled the runners from the box.

'They're huge!' I exclaimed.

'They said shoes need to be two sizes too big.'

'God, they're so long. I will look like a clown.'

'Well, that's what they told us you need. You don't want pressure sores,' she remarked. 'Oh, and I brought in some of your jumpers and T-shirts. You can choose which ones you like.'

'Yeah, OK.'

I would now be matching everyone else in the ward. It was obvious why tracksuit pants were recommended: they were more comfortable and easier to get on and off, especially for the nurses when cleaning me up after I crapped myself, which was inevitable as my body figured out how it now worked.

Following the 'shower of disappointment' and dressed in my new workout gear and the Adidas 'canoes' strapped to my feet, the nurse wheeled me down the gentle incline from the main building to the dining room, for breakfast. I didn't know it yet, but that small incline was going to be one of the biggest challenges I set for myself to conquer in the future.

A few of the stragglers were still there, mainly people with high-level quadriplegia who needed to be fed. We looked at each other across the table. I was curious but also aware of my own situation: Did I look like them? It was the first time I had seen other people up close in a wheelchair. One was in a power chair; two, who looked more disabled, were in recliner wheelchairs like me—which was probably how I looked—and one other was in what looked like a standard wheelchair. I wondered about their levels of disability, and they were probably thinking the same about me as the nurses shoved a piece of toast or a scoop of cereal in their mouths.

I hadn't put in a meal order, so it was whatever was left over.

'You can have toast or toast, David. What would you like on it?' the nurse asked.

'I'll have jam if there is any,' I replied. 'Could I have a coffee too?'

'I will see if I can get one.'

Cuppa Teeeaa was still rattling her way around the ward, so the nurse managed to get me a barely palatable lukewarm coffee.

'So, how'd ya snap it?' came a voice across the table from the power wheelchair.

'Came off a motorbike. You?' I said, as the nurse waved the cold toast in front of my mouth, waiting for the moment I stopped talking to shove it in.

'Car, rolled it three times,' he said.

Another nurse was feeding him, but he had awkward movements in his arms and floppy hands encased in weird leather glove-like things. His name was Gary and he was a 'quad,' meaning he had quadriplegia. People with paraplegia were called 'paras.' He'd been a quad for a few years, and was in temporarily for an operation. He was a C4/5, a level higher than me with only a little arm movement.

'What level are ya?' Gary asked.

'They tell me I'm C5 with some movement down to C6 or something,' I said.

'You'll be here a while then.'

'I suppose so.'

Each patient was assigned a primary nurse for the duration of their stay in rehab. She or he was responsible for teaching the patient all they needed to know about their care, such as medication, pressure sores and anything else that was a prerequisite to getting home and being able to 'just manage.'

As well as my ongoing education, the nursing staff had to educate my parents and family on my situation—what quadriplegia was, and what I would likely need. This was very important for them to be able to move forward. Having some knowledge, no matter how confronting, made the unknown a little clearer. Over the last two months, they'd had time to come to terms with my situation and understand that the change to their lives wouldn't be as dramatic as they'd first thought: Mum wouldn't need to quit her job to look after me, after all. My family would be able to move on from the trauma to a degree, and after my abrupt realisation the previous night, I was now ready to move forward and meet the challenges head-on.

After breakfast, I was introduced to my nurse, Thea. All the nurses dressed in casual clothes in Ward 17: Thea, in jeans and a white T-shirt, was a slim Greek girl with a longish face, wavy dark-brown hair and, like many nurses, was down to earth and practical. Thea was twenty-five years old, and we got along really well right from the start, which was important as there would be many questions I would need answered, including many personal ones.

'OK Dave, it's lunchtime. Time to start with your rehab,' Thea said.

'Oh, OK,' I said, not knowing what was in store for me.

The wheelchairs rolled into the dining room like cows meandering into the milking shed, some surprisingly quickly, manned by the more able patients, the remainder with nurses on the back pushing them in, like me.

In the dining room two large tables were placed end-to-end down the middle of the room, wheelchairs lining the perimeter. It was managed chaos with nurses running around parking wheelchairs, getting people and lunches organised, the sharp eye-squinting noise of cutlery being dropped on the vinyl floors reverberating in the room.

Thea flipped the covers off my lunch, exposing watery tomato soup, again—there must have been a sale on—some sort of casserole that didn't look too bad, and jelly and Two Fruits for dessert. With my personal nurse, getting fed would take a more leisurely pace, I thought. But the reality was not how I had imagined.

'OK, Dave, you need a Palm Pocket. Let's see if I can find one for you,' Thea said.

'A what?' A minute later she was back.

'This thing, this is a Palm Pocket. Are you left or right-handed?'

'Ah … I used to be right,' I said, a little bewildered as to what she was going to do.

After strapping the Palm Pocket band around my right palm, Thea grabbed a spoon and bent the head down thirty degrees to the handle, then stuck the spoon's handle into the narrow pocket sitting in my palm. 'OK, dig in!' she said, as she arranged the bowl within easy reach. I started with the soup.

The spinal cord is like a telegraph wire running down the middle of your neck and back, with branches coming off feeding the various parts of the body. Damage to the spinal cord is like damaging a telegraph line: the signal stops. Anything below the damaged section won't work, but anything above is still working. The lower the damaged section, the more movement you have above.

When I broke my neck, I obliterated the fifth cervical vertebra, breaking it into three pieces. Although I broke the fifth vertebra (C5) in my neck, I have some movement down to the next level, C6. My tactile sense—that is, what I can feel—is also closer to C6. I'm classified as C5/6 complete. The little bit of C6 that still works makes a difference in what I am able to do.

My injury has left me with no finger function at all. I have wrist extension, which means when my palm is facing down, I can raise the back of my hand towards the back of my forearm. But I have no wrist flexion—with my palm facing up, I can't raise my hand towards my forearm. I also have no movement below my armpits. My arm function is also limited: my biceps work, but triceps don't. If I lift my arm above my head it falls back down—makes it hard to pick my nose when I'm lying on my back!

I have relatively normal feeling around my shoulders and down to a little above my nipples and on the top sides of my arms down to my thumbs, but no feeling on the underside of my arms or hands. Unless you fully sever your spinal cord, some patchy sensation may remain such as, in my case, patches of dull sensation on my bum and feet.

One of the hardest things to manage with my disability is temperature control, as my body no longer regulates it. My body takes on the temperature of the environment: when it's hot I overheat, when it's cold I freeze. I'm just like a reptile.

I was later told by a specialist consultant who assessed my level of function, that I was 94 percent impaired. This leaves me with only around six percent of my physical function. The question of what six percent function actually meant; and what I would be able to do or experience in my life, was ever present in my mind.

According to Thea, I would be able to feed myself, although obviously it would be a challenge. Was this using six percent or four percent? If feeding myself would be a challenge, what else would I be able to do? Would it *all* be a huge challenge?

Taking a deep breath, I concentrated intensely as if I was Luke Skywalker summoning the 'Force' to will my heavy limb towards my soup. Like an overextended crane with a heavy load in high wind, my right arm weaved awkwardly from side to side as I reached out. With the bent spoon in my palm pointing out to the side between my forefinger and thumb, I plunged it into the plastic bowl of soup; actually, more of a drop than a coordinated scoop. Willing my arm up again, I concentrated as intensely as a brain surgeon, carefully lifting my shaking hand and bringing it back to my body, all the while trying desperately not to spill the meagre contents onto the table. As the spoon met my lips, I lost control for a split second, hitting my lip, with half the soup ending up in my mouth and the rest dribbling down my chin into my neck brace, the cottonwool soaking it up. Feeling a little despondent, I gave it another go, but again the result was just as futile.

Shit, that was so fuckin' hard, I thought. My arms worked, sort of, but I couldn't control them. I sat feeling frustrated and a little self-conscious about the food on my face.

Still, I was hungry, and I wasn't about to give up. Eyeing off another guy having a little more luck, I noticed that he aimed the spoon at the plate and scooped the food up like a charging front-end loader tractor.

OK, change of plan. Let's work on the casserole instead, I thought. With the focus of a highwire tightrope walker, I extended my arm out again, dropping it and driving it into the small mass of food, then raising it with a full load to mouth height. With a little more speed this time to steady my arm, I brought it closer. Bang! In it went, giving me a satisfying mouthful of food. Breathing a sigh of relief, I munched on the chewy substance and smiled: I had done it, I'd fed myself for the first time since my accident, and it tasted damn good. Albeit brief, it was my first feeling of achievement. But this was only the first one; I had many more mouthfuls to go.

Frustratingly, the contents of my casserole kept moving from one side of the plate to the other, trying to escape the spoon. But with Thea's skilful intervention of continually rotating the plate so I could attack it from the best direction, I managed to finish it.

It would take time, but eventually I would even conquer one

of the greatest Australian challenges—eating a hot, sloppy meat pie without getting it all over myself or third-degree burns on my fingers. Being able to do this without the use of fingers is a real accomplishment. The trick is, eat fast!

7

NEW WHEELS

I believe we all have a choice in everything we do: we are in control of our destiny. We may not like the consequences or outcomes of the options, but we still ultimately have a choice. Every decision we make now, or in the future, or made sometime in the past has a consequence—good, neutral or bad. It might not be a decision that immediately affects us, but it will at some stage, in ways we may never expect.

All the decisions I made on the day of the accident—going to work, then going out and deciding to jump onto the motorbike—led me to the point where I was now, with a broken neck, not knowing what my future would be. Maybe because of this—the fact that I had made those decisions—I could move towards accepting my situation, my fate, a little quicker than others I met at the Austin. I took responsibility for my situation. Don't get me wrong, I still felt acutely the loss of what I once had, what I could once do. I didn't want to be in this situation; I wished I had everything back so intensely, the frustration of not being able to do anything for myself was at times overwhelming. I couldn't change my situation, but what I could change was the way I dealt with it. We are all capable of choosing our attitude in any given situation and determining our way forward. It was now up to me to make the best of the situation, to choose my way. I could either decide to do my best and push myself to do as much as I could, or I could give up and let my life drift away.

All the simple things I took for granted—picking up a cup to take a drink, feeding myself, brushing my teeth, brushing my hair—all the basic things I'd done every day without thinking, I had to relearn with only six percent of physical function. How far would six percent go? I wanted to find out. I had made my decision.

During the week, I was booked in for my regular occupational therapy and physiotherapy sessions to start me on my journey of rehabilitation.

Once up in the morning, the physio assistant came to the ward to wheel me down to the gym. Benches about the size of a double bed, padded and covered in vinyl, were in the centre of the room. Vinyl foam-filled mats lay on the floor along one wall, and exercise equipment was positioned randomly along the other walls. A set of parallel bars were off to the side; they were for the patients who didn't do the job right and could still walk.

My physio, Tracey, a blonde English girl, was always smiling, even when I did my bad Michael Caine impersonation of an English accent.

The first thing I had to learn was balancing. Unable to move anything from my armpits down, the only way I can sit without support is by balancing using my arms and head. A bit like Humpty Dumpty, but hopefully without too much falling.

Tracey sat behind to prop me up as I tried to hold myself up in a sitting position with my legs out in front, balancing by waving my uncoordinated arms around and moving my head like the robot from *Lost in Space*. Although I never yelled, 'Warning! Warning!' It was 'Shit! Shit!'—as I kept falling over. It was exhausting—I only managed a couple of seconds at a time—but over the weeks I gradually improved until I could sit without Tracey holding me. This was a fundamental skill to acquire, especially when learning how to transfer from the wheelchair onto a bed, or even just sitting in a wheelchair without falling out.

Other patients were at various stages of their rehab. Some were independent, pulling heavy weights or leaping out of their wheelchairs onto the benches, practising transferring. At the other end of the spectrum, the lower-level quads tentatively tried to transfer onto the benches without overbalancing and face-planting the floor.

As I looked around, I wondered where I fitted in. Would I be able to do what they could? It all seemed so far away. I could barely balance sitting up, let alone get myself out of my wheelchair and lift my body onto a bench. I felt like the green recruit at boot camp; the experienced and strong ones around me were about to go off to battle the big wide world. I hoped I would get through and become one of them.

My two-month stay in bed had eaten away what little strength I had after the accident, and gym work was on the menu to build it up. I was strapped to various machines throughout the session to isolate and work the few muscles that still functioned.

One of the machines we all dreaded was the 'Coffee Grinder.' This was like an exercise bike for the arms. The unit sat on a table; on each side it had a handle or crank like a bike. Tracey tied my hands to it with bandages and I spent the next fifteen minutes rotating the handles for as long and as fast as I could without stopping. After a short rest I had to do it again. It was painful! My few remaining muscles would burn, turning to jelly in the process. Just when I thought it was getting easier, Tracey would turn up the resistance, making it harder again. I couldn't leave my post with my hands bandaged to the machine, so if I stopped for a breather Tracey would look over and say, 'I can't see you working, David!' Although the session was painful, at the end I knew I had worked hard, and I felt a real sense of achievement knowing I was doing my best and giving myself the best chance for my future.

I had been waiting a few weeks for the new wheelchair the hospital was providing so I could finally get out of the huge recliner. I was getting a silver Sibbings wheelchair with a high backrest to help with my crap balance, and blue vinyl upholstery. The design hadn't changed for the last fifty years, with its heavy steel frame and huge cast-iron footplates that a blacksmith could use for an anvil.

The first thing I wanted to do was push from the gym down to 13 East and say hi to the staff who'd looked after me a few weeks earlier. I wanted to show them my progress, and to reconnect with the people who'd cared for me over those months.

Following a few adjustments to the footplates for my long legs, a bandage around my waist to prevent an embarrassing face-slam and a couple of test pushes, Tracey gave me the OK and I was off, pushing towards the passage from the gym leading directly to 13 East with only one turn. My new wheelchair looked much sleeker than the Jason Recliner, but it was still very heavy, like an old Holden Kingswood. I had only done ten metres and I was exhausted. *Christ, I didn't think it would be this hard.* With muscles burning, I looked down the hall; I had another thirty long metres to go.

My heart sank a little more with each push as reality became clearer. *I'm not going to be zipping around anytime soon,* I thought. *If I'm struggling to push on the flat, how will I ever push up a small incline, or even go outside?* I didn't want to be beaten. I wasn't going to give up, but the little piece of hope I had for my future shrank a little more.

After a few more marathons with intermittent breaks to rest

my burning and weary muscles, I finally wheeled into 13 East: I had made it. The surprised and familiar faces came to greet me as I crossed my imaginary finish line. 'Hey pussy, great to see you up,' said Ray, one of the orderlies. It was a term of endearment as we stirred each other a little. We had a common interest; he used to be a carpenter like me, but gave it up when work dried up in the '80s.

All I had to do now was get myself back to the gym.

8

OCCUPATIONAL TORTURE

Each day, along with physio, I attended occupational therapy, which is a code word for 'ultimate frustration.' The OT room reminded me of a classroom. It was bright with the sun shining through the windows, storage cupboards around the perimeter, and three rows of tables with only a couple of chairs for the staff to use. Strange devices that looked like primitive games sat on some of the tables. They were games all right, but games of frustration.

On my first visit, Christine, my OT, introduced me to one of them. It was called the 'Nail Block.' As the name suggests, it was a board with rows of nails that extended about twenty-five millimetres out from the board. On each nail was a small cylindrical block. The purpose of this device was to practise picking up the little blocks with non-functioning fingers. Although I don't have any finger function, I have what's called tenodesis grip. This occurs when the palm of my hand is facing down, and by raising my hand towards the back of my forearm (wrist extension), the fingers close with the thumb providing a weak pinch grip with the pointer finger. The idea was to lift the little blocks off each of the nails, around twenty-five of them, and put them back on, over and over again.

Christine demonstrated what she wanted me to do. I tried to do the same with my right arm, dropping my hand down, lifting my hand up, fingers closing. *Good*, I thought. My fingers gripped the block, then I slowly lifted it up. 'Damn,' I muttered, as the block caught the top of the nail, my fingers losing grip, the block sliding back down the nail to where it started. Again, I willed in vain for my fingers to hold on to the block. The lack of sensation in my fingers made it hard to know if I had a good grip, sliding it up so carefully. *It's off!* The first one. I breathed out, enjoying a moment of relief and satisfaction.

I managed to get a couple more off, but by this time my arm and wrist had had it. It was exhausting, the concentration of willing my limbs to do tasks they were not used to, and my limbs fatigued so quickly.

At each session the board came out; over and over again, I practised taking the blocks off the nails and putting them on again. It was so infuriating: something so simple was so hard. Some days my fingers seemed to do what I wanted, but other days, nothing went right. I felt the frustration well up inside me, from fury to feelings of helplessness, holding back tears as I struggled to take the 'fuckin' things off.

As my wrists strengthened, my coordination improved and the hours of frustration yielded practical results. Being able to pick up a foam cup with water in it and taking a drink made all the hard work worth it.

Although occupational therapy was frustrating, it was also rewarding. Making cups of tea or coffee, or trying to work out how to hold a teabag or spoon for the sugar without functioning fingers, were small but significant challenges that I would eventually conquer. Using a Palm Pocket to eat with was clumsy, but as the strength in my wrist improved, Christine upgraded me to using a fork and spoon with a brass ring welded on the top. My thumb went through the ring and the handle of the fork or spoon slid between my pointer and middle fingers, allowing me to use cutlery that was easier and far more practical.

9

FIRST OUTING

As I hadn't seen the outside world for almost three months, my memories of what life used to be like were hazy and distant.

The Royal Melbourne Show was in full swing, and Sandy the recreation coordinator, who was a very able paraplegic following a car accident, put the word out that leave for the day could be arranged. We were going to the show!

I hadn't been since I was seventeen with Robyn who tried to set me up with a friend of hers. I wasn't interested, mainly because I liked Robyn at the time, although she did have a boyfriend.

Getting out of hospital for a day and breaking the monotony was exciting; I couldn't wait. Mum was also coming and was as clueless as I was about what to expect. Although she felt some apprehension, with staff accompanying us, some of her worry was alleviated. This would be an adventure for both of us.

It was shaping up to be an unusually hot day for late September, around thirty degrees with blue skies. There were around six patients with varying levels of disability and stages of rehab. A couple of the paras were getting ready for their departure from hospital to start their lives again. This outing was good practice to hone their wheelchair skills and experience the realities of the outside world.

Apart from the soon-to-leave paras, a staff member accompanied each quad to push us around and help with any medical emergency, such as emptying the bulging 'calf muscle' (leg-bag) before our urinary condoms exploded and we wet ourselves.

Carol, a trainee physio, and Mum escorted me: my first day back in the real world. With my neck brace on, Velcro strap around my waist to stop me falling out if the chair hit a small bump, tablets and catheters overflowing like a Christmas stocking in a bag hanging behind my chariot, we wheeled out and down the steep road to Heidelberg train station. Carol tilted my chair back in a fluid move so I didn't fall forward from the road's steep incline, surprising Mum. 'Are you OK, David?' she queried, instinctively putting a hand on my shoulder as the gradient increased, concerned that her son might break the land speed record if Carol slipped and let me go.

'Yes, I'm fine, Mum!' I said, not wanting to be mollycoddled, especially in front of Carol.

I felt a little envious as I watched the paras zigzagging down the road, having fun with the gravity, showing off their ability. Then Sandy shot past like a rocket, straight down the hill balancing on his back wheels all the way down, showing the others what was possible. It was exciting to watch, like a fast car race, just wondering who would crash first.

It was a totally new experience, and I had no idea how I was going to get around in the wheelchair. When the train rattled into the station and pulled up, Mum stood back as the staff transformed into a precision pit crew. Carol and another nurse lined me up backwards to the door and tilted the chair back, instantly levitating me up the step into the train. The remaining patients were all in within seconds before the doors slammed shut and the train lurched off. Carol caught me as I fell sideways, not ready for the jolt as the train pulled out of the station.

As the carriage rocked back and forth, I wrapped my forearm around a pole next to me to try to balance myself, Mum holding my chair to stop it from moving. The world now seemed very different; it felt strange. The train, the passengers, the scenery whizzing past the windows: it was all familiar, but so different. It was like going back to a house you lived in during your childhood, then returning as an adult. The memories, the smells, the sights—it all felt like a lifetime ago.

How we experience the world depends on each person's circumstances. I wasn't sure how I felt or how to react as I noticed a few passengers looking at me, then when I looked at them, quickly glancing away as if caught staring at something they shouldn't. I wasn't being noticed because of my six-foot-three height towering over people; rather, heads turned to look at a disabled person in a wheelchair. Also, I was now staring at people's bums as they stood, which wasn't so bad when I had a nice female bum to look at. The world had changed because my circumstances had changed: I was now experiencing it sitting down.

At the show, we split up and agreed to meet up at the station at 3 p.m. for the train back to the Austin.

It was soul-reviving to be outside in the sunshine and warmth, but there were so many people. Carol drove me into a gap in a slow-moving queue. The bum ahead, or the oncoming breasts and crotch, were all I could see in the sea of humanity. I felt nervous as Carol drove the heavy cast-iron footplates of my chair perilously close to the heels of the man ahead.

Suddenly the unsuspecting victim stopped. Smash! My footplates slammed into him, taking his foot out from underneath and a few layers of skin as a souvenir. I even felt it, his face wincing with pain as he tried to right himself while holding his ankle, gathering his rage to hurl abuse at the perpetrator: me. 'Sorry mate,' I said, as he looked up. The expression of anger suddenly changed when he saw me in my wheelchair, neck brace and Velcro seat belt. 'Ah, sorry mate,' he said, then quickly hobbled off, catching up with the person ahead. I felt bad and was really annoyed with Carol, but there were obviously advantages to being a quad. The Quad Card!

We wandered around the show. I made sure Carol kept her distance from people, and Mum mastered pushing the heavy chair and tilting it back over the bumps without throwing me out. It soon became apparent there really wasn't much I could do. I couldn't go on the rides, and Carol wasn't about to let me loose in the beer hall, no matter how much I nagged.

'How about the cattle pavilion?' Mum suggested.

'If we have to,' I grumbled as she pushed me towards it. Entering the building, the overpowering acrid smell of urine, manure and hay slapped me in the face. Huge beasts of different breeds mooed and stared at me with curiosity as Mum rolled me past the stalls. Halfway down, bits of hay and green stuff were flicking up off the wheels.

'Oh no, I have crap on me!' I said.

'You have what?' said Mum.

'Cow shit. I'm covered in cow shit!'

'Don't worry David, it's just a bit of manure,' said Mum, being her matter-of-fact self.

'Argg... it's disgusting!' I said, unable to get away from it.

With some urgency, Mum pushed me a little faster to get outside quickly. As the wheels gathered speed, bits of cow shit mixed with straw flicked up higher onto my pants and to the side of my T-shirt like a sprinkler system.

With my sunburnt face and arms, and cow shit-stained clothes, we wearily trained it back to the Austin. The depleted paras needed a push up the hill, their overzealous attitudes brought back to earth as the huge hill loomed in front of them. Mum and Carol were exhausted from pushing me all day, and I was drained from the day's experience. I hadn't known what to expect, nor had Mum, but she took it all in her stride. It was a great adventure, giving us a taste of what reality outside my secure environment might be like. It wasn't as scary or difficult as I'd first thought but, no doubt, it would be challenging. A few more pieces of the puzzle of what my life was going to become were put in position, adding to the others I had already placed.

10

MANHOOD

One question that is usually on people's minds, although they are too embarrassed to ask, is: Can people with quadriplegia get an erection? Generally, yes. But for most, it doesn't work the same way it used to. I can't think a sexy thought and get it up. It works on reflex—rub it like a genie's lantern and it will grow like bamboo in the tropics.

Following my bladder performance test, with the discovery that I had high pressure when my bladder contracted, which if left untreated could eventually damage my kidneys, the spinal doctor paid me a little visit to tell me the 'good' news.

'David, the pressures are a little high in your bladder and it is recommended that you have a sphinctorotomy.'

'A sphincta…whatomy?' I said.

He explained why I needed the procedure, which sounded fairly reasonable for someone in my situation; and being young, I didn't want renal failure until I was old, around fifty or so.

'It's a standard procedure, we make some small cuts to the sphincter at the outlet of the bladder,' he reassured me. In reality, it is like jabbing a Bamix against the sphincter, mincing it to pieces, a nurse later told me in graphic detail that made me squirm.

'David, there are some risks. A very slight chance you could die.'

Well, they say that to everyone, and it didn't bother me.

'Also, there is a chance you could lose the ability to have an erection.'

'What? Lose my erection?' *No way! That's the last piece of manhood I have left*, I thought in my moment of shock as I tried to process what he was telling me.

'Why? Do I really need the operation?' I asked.

I knew it was logical for me to have it, but to lose my pillar of manliness; that was a sacrifice I really didn't want to think about.

I didn't care about the other risks: death, ha, that didn't mean anything to me. However, my erection was the last thing I had left that sort of worked as it did when I was an 'upright.' It's not that I was looking to have sex with anyone, and I wasn't even sure I'd find someone who'd want to have sex with me. But I had lost so much; I didn't want to lose any more. I didn't want my life made any harder, and I wanted to keep what few remnants of normality I could. And it's damn handy when it comes to putting on condom drainage.

I didn't like the choices, but whatever my future, I knew what it had to be.

Feeling cold and groggy from the operation and anaesthetic, bedridden for the next week as I waited for my Bamixed sphincter to heal enough so the garden-hose-sized catheter could be removed, my mind cleared. I lay wondering: *Does it work?*

Later that night, one of the nurses came in to wash me and give everything a good check, making sure the catheter was still flowing 'Rosé' with a mixture of blood and urine. I felt a little embarrassed but had to know: 'Ah, is it OK down there?' I queried. Without having to be too specific, she knew what I wanted to know. She had probably been asked this question many times.

'I think you will be OK, David,' she said.

11

AN IDLE MIND IS THE DEVIL'S WORKSHOP

Apart from watching TV, there was a lot of time sitting around, so to speak. On a sunny day we'd park ourselves in the covered area between the accommodation building and the lunchroom, or out the front, and enjoy the afternoon sun and chat, surveying the coming and going of people. A few paras were smokers. I guess, without the trauma of having a trachy, they took up their habit where they left off once out of the acute ward. My two-month stay in bed was a rebirth as a non-smoker with very clean lungs, and I really didn't miss it.

But as the saying goes, 'An idle mind is the devil's workshop,' and with hours of boredom on my hands and smokers around me, temptation started to rear its ugly head. Of course, I knew better; but with my pneumonia, a collapsed lung, a tracheostomy, and the months of chest physio now well in the past, one puff wouldn't hurt.

I scored a cigarette off Ron in the TV room, one of the paras who wasn't much shorter in the wheelchair than when he was an 'upright.' He was a jockey before a horse took a dislike to him being on its back.

'Hey Linda, can I have a light?' I asked one of the nurses as she walked past in the outside covered area. I knew from the stern look that she did not approve.

'I will give you a lighter, but I won't light it for you. You shouldn't be smoking with your lung capacity, David,' she said.

With the lighter resting in my non-functioning fingers in my gummy hands, Linda gave a smile and walked away knowing that I couldn't use it.

Hmm, was that a challenge? I thought. I sat wondering how I could work the mechanism. It was the standard Bic type with a roller to spark the flint with the thumb, and a small lever the thumb holds down to keep it alight. I experimented with various positions to hold the lighter, using different fingers to try and roll the roller to get a spark, but nothing worked.

Linda came back to see how I was going, hoping I had given up. 'Still trying, David?' she asked.

'Getting there,' I said, not raising my head as I was fixated on the task at hand.

Stephan rolled out the door and parked himself next to me, slouching forward with one arm hanging onto the push handle at the back of the wheelchair. 'What you doing, Dave?' he said, intrigued by my endeavour to spark the lighter.

'Trying to light this thing. Not happening though,' I said.

He offered some suggestions that I had already attempted, then watched in amusement as I kept trying.

I ran an idea through my mind: *OK, if I just make a fist with my fingers, push the lighter between my pointer and middle fingers so the base rests on my palm... That works! If I can't use my fingers, what else will work to spin the roller? The heel of my palm!*

As I struck down on the roller with the heel of my palm, sparks spat with a little waft of smoke. 'Aww!' Stephan said, getting excited. My heart started racing with the increased chance of it actually working. I hit the roller again, more sparks, but I didn't get the heel of my hand onto the little lever to let the gas flow. 'Almost! You almost got it!' said Stephan. Flick, sparks, flash—a flame appeared briefly, the heel slipping off the lever. 'Wow, yeah!' We both gave a cheer at my split second of success.

It was exciting for both of us. Stephan was at the same level as me—we were both relearning how to do some of the simple things we had lost. If I could do it, then he would likely be able to do it too. Smoking wasn't what was important; it was the sense of achievement and knowing that a little more independence and freedom was possible. One more task crossed off the very long 'Can't Do' list.

I gave it another go, then another and another. Flash! The lighter burst to life and stayed on. 'Aw, ha-ha, woohoo!' we cheered, laughing at each other as if we had played a hilarious practical joke on someone. In this case, the joke was on Linda. I held up the burning flame like the Olympic torch, wearing a grin from ear to ear. I had succeeded when I didn't know if it was possible. I was not beaten.

12

CONFRONTING

Daphne was a friend I hadn't seen in a long time, not since before my accident. I got to know her through my best mate Pete, and she lived around the corner from me in Glen Waverley. She was a genuine and lovely person, slim and attractive with olive skin, shoulder-length brown hair and a warm smile. I hadn't expected her to visit me, but it was a nice surprise when she turned up one evening.

When she walked in, I felt a little uncomfortable lying naked under the blankets, with my shoulders bare. Her warm smile lit up the room and I was pleased to see her.

So she wouldn't get the wrong impression and think I was one of 'those' quadriplegics you might see on TV who spent their whole life in bed, I quickly explained that I was usually up in my wheelchair, and I was only in bed as I couldn't get myself in at this point. Visitors were usually allowed to stay until around 9 p.m., but I still had to be in bed by 7.30 p.m. so the afternoon staff could get organised and do their handover to the night staff.

Daphne had recently come back from a few months' holiday in Greece visiting her relatives. We chatted about what my days were like (not that anything changed much from my regular program, unless something exciting like a different meal was served), who was doing what, her holiday, and what she had been up to since I last saw her.

She then showered me with presents from her trip: a watch, T-shirt and lots of things that I really didn't have much use for at the time. It seemed a little out of the ordinary, but it was really nice to be spoilt. *Maybe this quad thing could work for me?* I thought.

Pumpkin hour arrived so fast; the nurse popped her head into my room to say it was nine o'clock and time for visitors to leave. 'Thanks for coming in, Daph, it was great to see you. And thanks for all the pressies,' I said.

'That's OK. It was great to see you too. Take care, Dave, and I'll see you again soon,' she said, then kissed me goodbye, gave me a hug, and I watched her walk out of the room. That was the last time I ever saw her.

I have always wondered why she never came back. Did she find it too hard, too much of a shock? Some people who visited me found the experience very confronting. In contrast to the tall, strong and able person they'd known, seeing a skinny, weak-bodied person with limbs that looked funny and didn't work right was maybe too hard for some.

This didn't make me angry or resent Daphne, or anyone else for that matter. I guess we all deal with situations in different ways, whether it's joking around, being quiet and saying little, talking about the good old days or giving presents. If anything, I felt a little disappointed that she wouldn't see me in a less confronting situation, when I didn't look so disabled and she could see that I was still the same person.

I dealt with my situation in my own way too. I had had a lot of time to become accustomed to my circumstances, to my new life, even though it was changing every day the more I learnt. I was encapsulated in my cocoon, dealing with things the way I needed to, absorbed in my daily challenges. I guess I never gave much thought to how others were dealing with it at the time. I had the toughest role, didn't I?

Although early on my family was devastated by the accident, they were always supportive and positive, just very matter-of-fact about what was happening and letting it unfold without sorrow or blame. This positive attitude made it easier for me, not having to deal with other people's negative emotions, so I could focus all my mental and physical energy on what I was going through. My family is generally quite pragmatic, moving with the ebbs and flows of life, which is also characteristic of me.

13

SIBERIA

Two months in at Ward 17, the usual swabs of noses and groins were taken for testing to see who had the dreaded Golden Staph. I'd had mine done several times before with negative results, so I didn't give it a second thought.

'David, your swab is positive. You're going to be moved to the quarantine area,' the nurse said.

At the rear of Ward 17 was a room known as Siberia, the quarantine area. Anyone who was touched by the lowly plague was segregated from the rest of the 'healthy' patients, although we still ate and associated with everyone during the day.

I was banished! Gussy the orderly packed all my stuff, wearing plastic gloves and apron—which I thought was a little dramatic—and I was duly deported with the new ritual of having my groin and the inside of my nose painted with a purple liquid each morning.

Four patients were in Siberia, as that was all the beds they had. I'm sure there were other plague-infested individuals, but we were the unlucky ones this time.

Stephan was next to me; he was eighteen but came across as quite young, and was fairly quiet. He liked to chat about music, although the techno stuff he liked wasn't my scene. Scott in the adjoining room was a para who showed somewhat unusual behaviors and was a serious chain-smoker. He ended up at the Austin as a paraplegic following a stay at another hospital. Dribbling like a leaky tap down his food-stained T-shirt from the concoction of drugs he was on, Scott laughed with delight as he told me how he threw himself out of the hospital room window, smashing through the roof and landing on a table in the lunchroom, in front of the doctor who was apparently looking after him. I wasn't sure how true it was, but he did tell a good story.

Next to Scott, Paul was a white-haired, quiet, older gentleman of around sixty with paraplegia. He had a back operation which didn't go so well and was committed to a wheelchair for the rest of his life.

Shortly after I had arrived at Ward 17, a nurse said to me, 'You leave your dignity at the door and pick it up on the way out.' With only one large bathroom in Siberia, a toilet at one end, a basin in the middle section and the shower at the other end, it was a logistical endeavour to coordinate who got up when, mainly dependent on who had to go to the day's programs first. If we all had to go to the toilet on the same day, it was a very slow-moving production line.

Going to the toilet with a spinal injury involves much more than sitting on the dunny, pushing it out, then feeling light and refreshed after ten minutes or so. Now it was a much more involved and slower process which took about an hour or more. Let's be honest: we all like a good poo, and I really missed the ease and relief I'd feel after a good fast evacuation. It was now a tedious and tiring chore, every second day.

After Linda the nurse had inserted a suppository up my bum while I was in bed, and the orderlies had then lifted me onto the commode, with only a towel on my lap, I was wheeled into the smoky bathroom and parked in front of the basin and mirror. Scott was dragging on his cigarette, not paying any attention to the towel slipping off his lap. 'Hi Dave,' he said, looking up as Tony, the orderly, locked my brake and checked that the plastic bowl under the commode was central so as to catch the soon-to-be deposit.

'Hi Scotty, having a good crap?' I asked.

His dribbling smile said it all.

All four of us were lined up on our commodes—Scott first, then Stephan in the toilet section. I was in the middle area at the basin, and Paul behind me in the shower area.

Linda poked her head in. 'Dave and Paul, do you want a cuppa?' she asked.

'Yep. Coffee with lots of milk and one sugar, thanks, Linda,' I said.

'Can I have a cup of tea please?' Paul asked politely.

'Righto!' Linda was off to chase down the screeching and rattling tea lady we could hear at the other end of the ward.

The bathroom was like a bad smog day in China; we were invariably enveloped in the smoky haze from Scott's constant smoking.

'Can I have a smoke, Tony?' I asked. He pulled two out of his pack for Stephan and me, lit both up and stuck them in our mouths, the first drag giving me a serious head spin.

Paul didn't smoke, so he was relegated to behind me in the shower area.

'Here's your cuppa, Dave,' Linda said, turning the plastic-insulated cup around so I could slide my thumb into the handle like a hook to hold it. 'Can you take the smoke?' I asked, pursing my lips for her to remove the cigarette so as not to drop it in my lap, which would require some quick explaining to the charge nurse as to how I got burns on my groin.

A cigarette and hot cuppa first thing in the morning wasn't the healthiest, but it was an efficient way to speed up the process and get my bowels to move like a cement mixer expelling its load.

The smoke and noxious fumes would have made the average

person gag, but over time we all became very comfortable with it. The occasional muffled thud of the lonely deposit hitting the plastic bowl under the commode, followed by the echo of a wet 'thwaaarp' indicating a job well done, would crudely interrupt our in-depth conversations. It became a sport, with real-time commentary on each person's effort and commitment to the job, with a complex scoring system of flow rate, consistency and finish.

'I think I'm almost finished, Linda, can I have a check,' I said to nurse Jelly Finger. Linda promptly slapped on a glove, liberally smeared K-Y Jelly on her pointer finger, and proceeded to bury her finger up my bum-hole, rotating it in small circles to stimulate the bowel to expel anything high up. With nothing coming down, she rammed it all the way up. 'It's clear!' she said as she whipped out her finger and held it up like a prized trophy for inspection. My nod confirmed a good result.

Not wasting time, she pulled out the bowl so I could check my deposit. I keenly surveyed the specimen, trying to match its formation with the poo consistencies chart. 'Maybe you need a little more fruit,' Linda commented.

The first one to finish got wheeled into the shower for a quick splash, then back to bed for dressing, breakfast, and off to the days program.

Dad and me skiing at Mt Bachelor, Oregon, USA in 1979. This is where my love of downhill skiing began.

There was nothing better than hurtling down the streets on our billy carts: or in this case, at a much slower pace, with a converted motorized lawn mower on the back, age 11.

At 13 years, I loved motorbikes and looked forward to visiting my uncle and aunt's farm in Western Victoria to race around the back paddocks on the Honda CT 125.

Trying hard to do a modelling pose for my friend, Tanya, for her photography portfolio in 1988. *Photo: Tanya Carter*

Surfing at Smiths Beach, Victoria, in 1987. Friends and I would regularly head down to the coast on weekends, surf all day, then replenish our energy on dim-sims, hot chips and Coke on the drive home. *Photo: Rebecca Burt*

Relaxing after a surf at Smiths Beach, Victoria, in 1987.
Photo: Rebecca Burt

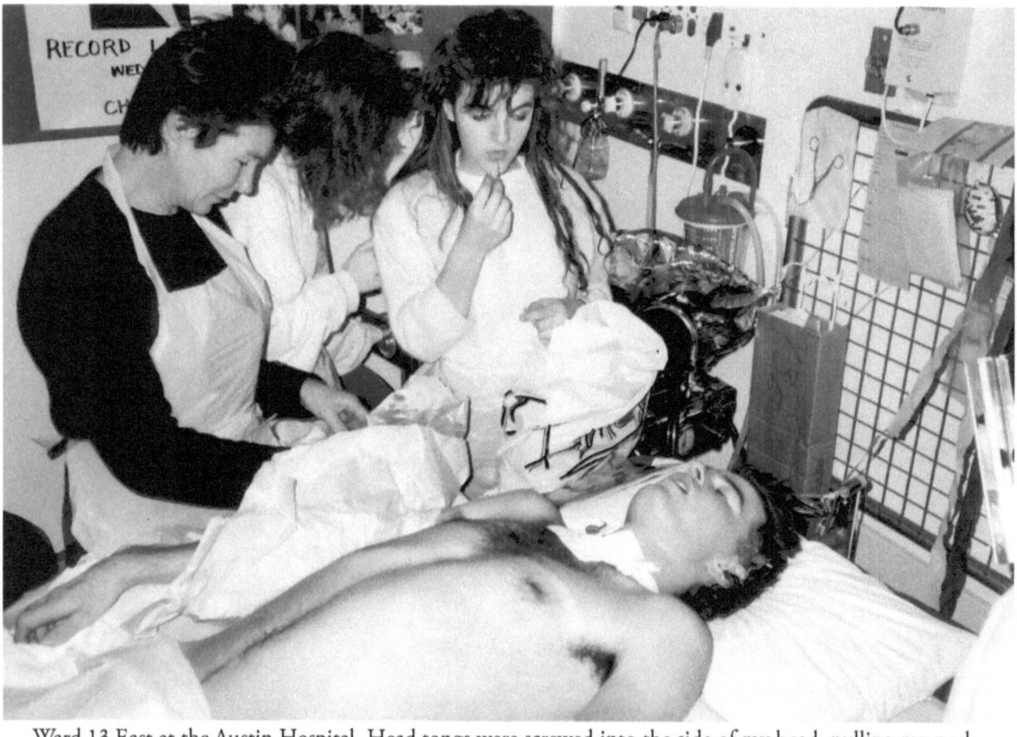

Ward 13 East at the Austin Hospital. Head tongs were screwed into the side of my head, pulling my neck straight, so the vertebrae could heal. This was the day I got my voice back and could again taste food when my trachy was blocked off (red cap blocks the hole). To celebrate, Mum brought in my favourite dinner, fish 'n' chips. Mum is on the left with my friend Tanya to the right, stealing a chip.

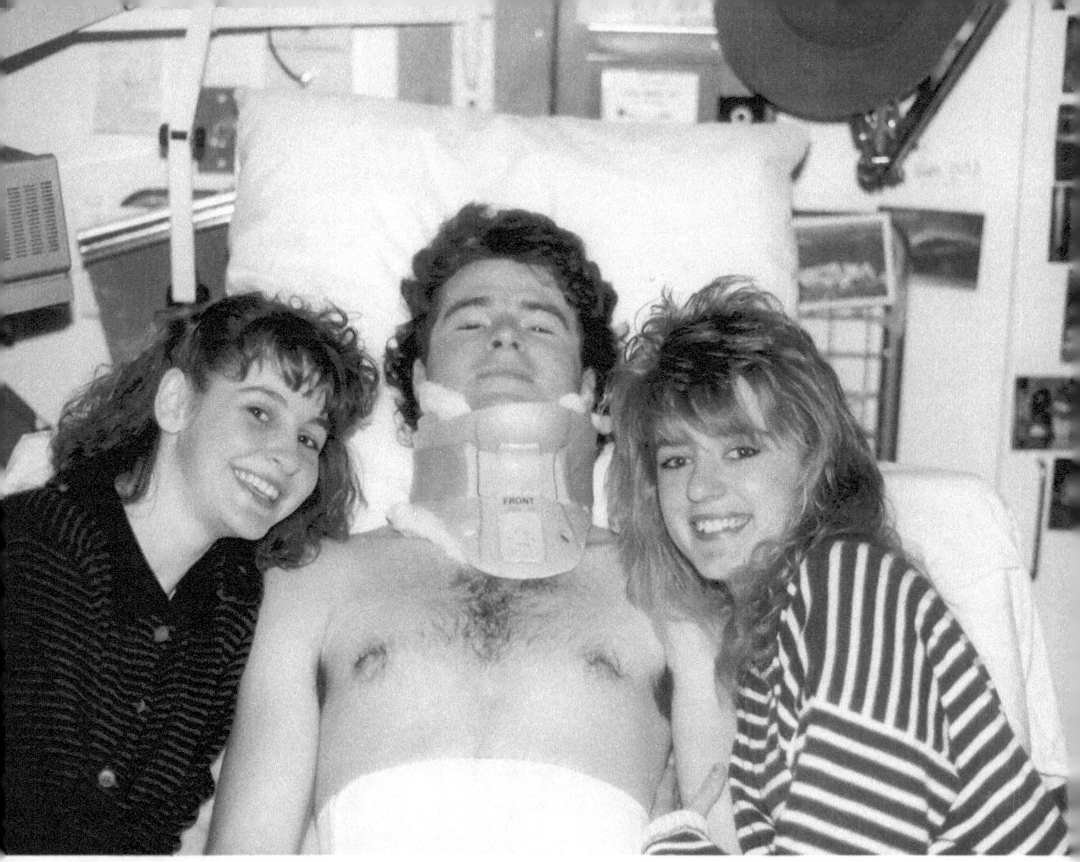

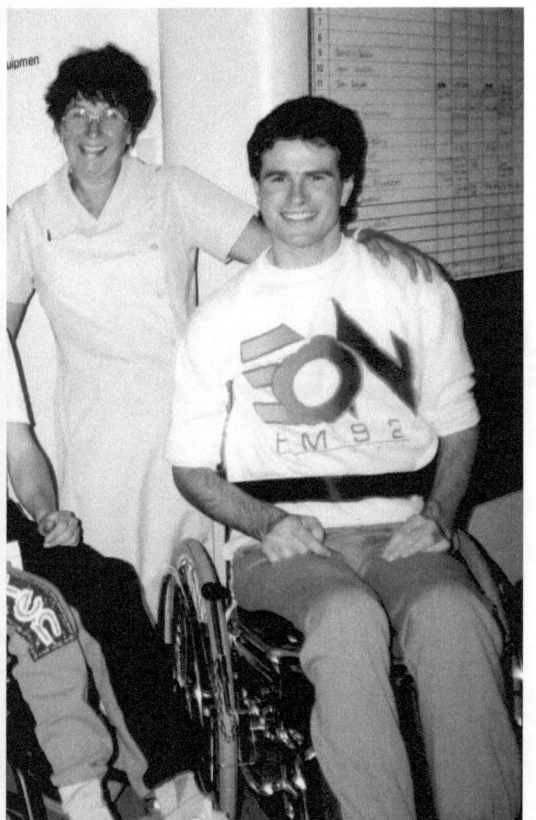

After almost two months the head tongs were removed and I started mobilisation—gradually being sat up in bed. The collar helped support my weak neck. I was so happy that I was on the path to getting my life back and that my friends and family could see that I was still me. Becky, me and Robyn.
Photo: Rebecca Burt

Me and Wilma, one of the awesome staff in Ward 17 during rehabilitation. I'm in my new Sibbings wheelchair with blue upholstery and a Velcro seat belt to stop me falling out, and decked out in the classic quad uniform—tracksuit pants.

Fork with Palm Pocket

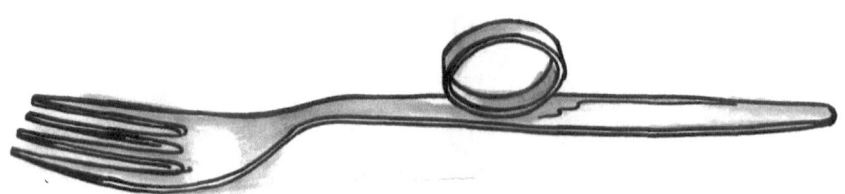

Fork with brass ring

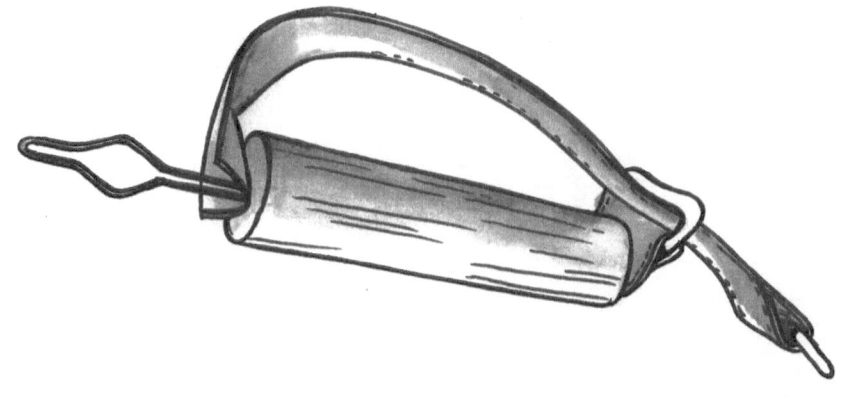

Button Hook

Wooden cutting board with swivel knife

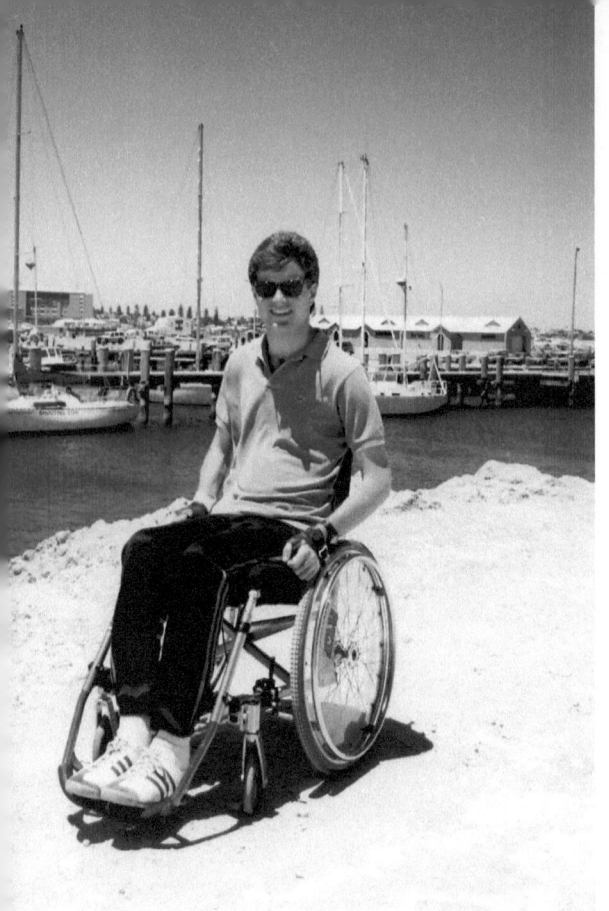

I'd lost a lot of weight during hospital and rehabilitation. It was great to be out in the community, getting back into life. Looking cool in my new Ray-Ban sunglasses and a new, flash, lightweight wheelchair.

Zak, my Blue Heeler dog and best mate, sitting on my lap eyeing off a bit of turkey at a family Christmas lunch. He'd do anything for food—even wear a silly Christmas hat!

14

BREAKING OUT

Life in rehab soon became very routine. We were woken at 7 a.m., usually by the screech of 'Cuppa teaah,' with the nurses and orderlies getting me up within two hours, by the end of which I was usually feeling a little worn out.

'OK, you're done, see you at lunch,' the nurse said as I went off to get my breakfast in the dining room, usually cereal or, with a little help to spread the topping, toast and a coffee.

After breakfast I was usually booked into physio around 10 a.m. For the next hour or so, I spent my time working out on the dreaded Coffee Grinder, practising transferring or rolling, then usually a weights session in the afternoon.

After a leisurely lunch from noon to around 1.30 p.m., Hans the Austrian OT assistant would promptly arrive and push me down the steep winding path I couldn't negotiate in my wheelchair to the OT building, adjacent to the gym. 'Who wants a cuppa?' I'd ask, offering Christine or Sue, the OTs, a microwaved tea, in the hope that my initiative to improve my tea-making skills might get me out of lifting the dreaded blocks.

If Mum, Dad or any other visitor didn't drop by in the afternoon, we usually had plenty of time on our hands waiting for dinner, with little else to do besides sit in the TV room or outside with other patients, smoking and talking. 'Nice chair!' someone would say, then the conversation would stop and eyebrows raise as we checked out the new chair.

'How does it handle?' someone asked.

'Yeah, good on the flat, a little tippy up a hill though,' demonstrating by popping the chair on its back wheels and showing off with a mono.

'What's it weigh?'

'Don't know. But it's light, ay!'

After kicking the tyres, so to speak, the conversation would turn to more important matters like the cricket, footy, what we would do when we were out of here; or someone would call out, 'Who wants to order pizza?' when the dinner menu wasn't looking appetising.

A new person coming through would spark our curiosity: everyone had a story. Some had sad stories, like Paul following a botched operation; others were more entertaining like one of the new paras. 'Yeah, I was on my honeymoon in Bali and fell backwards off the balcony. Broke my back. When I was flown back to Australia a week later, I still had sand in my hair,' he explained.

'But did you get a root?' someone blurted. It seemed pretty funny at the time.

I don't recall anyone saying, 'Why me?' We were all in the same boat with similar but different challenges, and I think this commonality made it easier for each of us to feel less alone. Some were better off than others, but in the end, it was just the luck of the draw as to how it turned out. We all secretly wished we had been a little luckier and got a little more function. Occasionally you'd hear a high-level quad say jokingly, 'God, I wish I had your triceps!' when a para transferred from his wheelchair onto the couch.

Speaking of paras: they were particularly handy for the quads when we needed a pair of functioning fingers. 'Can you pick up my smokes?' or 'Can you cut up my meal?' or 'Can you butter my toast?'

The paras were more than happy to share their dexterous fingers.

Their physical strength and ability were also useful. On more than one occasion, when a staff member wasn't around and I got stuck trying to push up the incline from the dining room to the main building, I'd hail a passing para. They would happily oblige by wheeling in behind my chair, locking the front of theirs into my rear, and with a boost, I could get to the top.

The small incline was only one of the physical barriers limiting my independence. Ward 17 became known as Stalag 17 to me and other higher-level quads. Perched at the top of a steep hill, it was near impossible for the less physically able to escape the geographical prison, except to the flat area of the rear carpark.

Following a bit of grumbling, Tracey upgraded my heavy Sibbings wheelchair to a red lightweight chair which made pushing much easier. With a little extra mobility, I soon had my ticket to freedom after finding an escape route from the ward. When the long passage past the nurses' station was clear, with each strained push on the wheels I slowly made my way to the lift at the rear. In my mind I had cunningly outsmarted the nurses, although in reality, at my pace I'm sure they had seen me and knew exactly where I was going.

It was the lift I had first come up in all those months ago: the musty smell and rattle was unmistakeable as it lowered me to the abandoned ward below. Making my way through the eerie empty corridors, I was half expecting the torso of a ghost to drift by. Through the underground tunnel leading to the main building, I was back in another lift that brought me up to ground level, rolling out onto the flat courtyard with a café. There was also a dodgy hairdresser: I got my first haircut since my accident, resulting in slick gelled sides and a serious mullet that Billy Ray Cyrus would have been proud of. I was not happy, although Stephan seemed to be quite pleased with his.

I hated being told I had to go to bed at 7 p.m. It made me feel as though I was no longer an adult, but most of all I mourned the loss of independence. If you could get into bed yourself, then you went when you wanted. I couldn't get myself out of my wheelchair, let alone into bed, therefore the afternoon staff corralled us all, tucking us away by 7.30 p.m. before handover to the nightshift staff. Most nights I'd watch TV, and if a wandering para rolled by, I'd get him or her to change the channel. The night staff usually dropped around soon after 9 p.m. for tablet distribution and to turn us over; then it was off to sleep.

Having to rely on people to do most things for me was very disempowering, but to have no choice about when I could go to bed took the last skerrick of freedom and independence away. However, if you could arrange for someone to put you to bed then you had a way out. I got to know Debbie, one of the less regular night nurses, quite well, so on occasion she would put me to bed, enabling me to stay up as late as I wanted, although it usually wasn't much past 9 p.m. anyway. I felt free, being able to roll around the quiet corridors, chatting to some of the other late-nighters, usually the paras. I felt I had a little more control over my life, even just for that moment.

With the warmer summer weather and progress with my rehab, I took every opportunity to go on the few outings that the ward offered, escaping the routine and experiencing my new world for a short time.

With each adventure I gained a little more insight into my life using a wheelchair, and some of the environmental challenges. My first trip into the city was a big event for many of us. The few paras were independent and planned to explore the town on their own. The rest of us less independent patients had to have someone to give us a push.

Janine was with me for the day. She was in her late twenties and had a relaxed but dry sense of humour which seemed to be a fairly common trait with nurses, really down to earth and great fun. She had looked after me in the ICU. On the first morning, as she bent over me with a face mask, bloodshot eyes and '40s hairstyle and said, 'Hi David, I'm Janine and will be looking after you today,' our friendship clicked straight away. I really enjoyed her company and, fortunately for me, she was now doing a nursing placement in rehab.

Again, it was a train into the city, then the various groups went their separate ways. Janine and I and a couple of others decided to go to the flatter part of the city, Bourke Street Mall, to check things out.

My lightweight wheelchair had a mind of its own as I strained to push it on the walkway up Swanston Street, all the time slowly turning towards the gutter due to the sloping path. I'd do a few small pushes, then have to straighten it back up and start again, making little progress. 'You're doing well, David,' Janine would say for encouragement, but I didn't feel I was, given such slow progress. With everyone else ahead in the distance, Janine had to give me a push to catch up.

'I wonder if the record store has a lift,' I said to Janine as I eyed off the escalator leading to the second floor.

'Why not use the escalator?' she said.

'What are you talking about?' I said.

'You can use the escalator with a wheelchair!'

'Really? Have you done it before?' I asked.

'No, but I've heard you can,' she said. This didn't fill me with confidence. I don't mind taking risks, but when I'm not in control, or at least think I am not in control, I get a little nervous.

If I remember correctly, one of the physios came with us. 'I can show you,' she said.

'Oh, OK,' I said, feeling a little more confident since she appeared to know what she was doing, as Janine pushed me towards the escalator.

'OK, it's pretty simple. All you have to do is wheel the casters onto the first step of the escalator. As it moves up, push the chair forward so the back wheels slot into the next step. Once it's on, hold the chair by pushing forward so Dave doesn't roll back,' she explained to Janine as she demonstrated the movement, pulling me back before I took off.

'If anything happens, just roll the chair off,' said the physio with reassurance.

I nodded in approval. 'Do you want to give it a go, David?' asked Janine.

'Yeah, OK. Just make sure you hold me.'

'Of course I will, don't you worry!' she said with a smile.

As Janine lined me up at the bottom of the escalator, the steps suddenly seemed to be going much faster.

'Go whenever you want Janine,' said the physio.

Janine moved me forward, and my front casters rolled onto the moving step, hitting the back of the rising one in front and stopping. As the front of my chair rose up, angling the backrest further back, I couldn't sit forward, my head falling into Janine's chest as the angle steepened before the rear wheels locked into the next step, and we started moving up.

It was an unnerving feeling, as I couldn't sit forward and instead was forced to lay back, putting all my trust in Janine.

Upon reaching the top, the chair flattened out and I rolled off onto the second level. I felt pretty chuffed that I could go on an escalator, although I still had to rely on another person. This piece of the jigsaw added to the larger picture of how I could manage in the outside environment. By this time, I had lost interest in the record store and was keen to see how I got back down, which was the same process, but it meant backing onto the escalator instead of going forward.

For many of us, a highlight of our time in the rehab unit was when Sandy organised a few outings to concerts at the tennis centre (now the Rod Laver Arena) in Melbourne. The advantage of being in wheelchairs was that we got fairly good seats, with the wheelchair spaces on the middle-tier walkway. It was a logistical challenge having to coordinate a dozen wheelchairs on the train, with most of the staff volunteering their time to help. Watching from afar, the line of wheelchairs resembled a rolling centipede as we weaved along the footpath from Flinders Street station to the arena.

Each time we went out I learnt something new, whether it was how to access the venues, what to tell people about my disability and needs, how difficult it was to find an accessible toilet, or getting a little more comfortable with the looks from other people—although I liked to think the girls thought I was a bit of all right and it wasn't the wheelchair they were looking at. We invariably had a great night, but after the concert it was usually a rush to catch the last train. If we missed it, we'd have a big problem—as I was about to find out with Virginia.

I had met Virginia when I was in 13 East. She was one of the nurses who had looked after me during the week, and we had struck up an instant rapport. She was quick-witted—although I was more of a smart-arse—we had a lot of fun together and we both liked the Rolling Stones. Mick Jagger was performing a concert later in the year, and I was hoping to go if I was mobile enough by then. When I mentioned this to Virginia, she said, 'If you need someone to go with you, let me know. I'd love to see him too.'

I scored some tickets and, good to her word, Virginia took me to the Mick Jagger concert with my mate Dave. It was the best night since my accident and Mick played the classics, my favourite being 'Paint It Black.' The concert went on for a long time and, in the excitement, we lost track of time, missing the last train to the hospital. We were stranded.

Virginia was very worried, and rightly so, as I wasn't allowed to travel by car because my neck was still considered unstable; the theory was that a sudden jolt could potentially damage my neck again, whereas in a train the risk was lower. If I did have to ride in a car, I had to wear a neck brace, but I didn't have one with me. Without any other options, Virginia called the hospital and it was agreed that I could go back in a taxi.

A taxi! I thought. Most of them are dangerous drivers; if I was at risk of damaging my neck, it was in a taxi.

'How about Dave driving us back. It'd be safer,' I said.

'No, it's got to be a taxi, David.'

After Virginia put immeasurable fear into the taxi driver that the slightest jolt would break my neck again, we took off for the Austin. I sat in the front seat with Virginia in the back, leaning forward and holding my head in her hands. 'Watch the bumps, slow down, slow down!' she barked at the poor taxi driver.

It was the slowest and most careful taxi ride I've ever had. I doubt he ever took another wheelchair user again.

15

LITTLE GOALS = HOPE

A lot was happening behind the scenes at home while I was in hospital. My parents were trying to get an extension built with a new bedroom and wheelchair-accessible bathroom at the back of their house for me to live in when I got out. During visits we often talked about the new room, a conversation I enjoyed as it was going to be mine, and building was what I did until six or so months ago.

'David, I have something to show you,' Dad said, pulling out a large piece of folded paper and opening it up.

'What is it?'

'It's the corner vanity to go in your new bathroom,' he said.

'God, it's big!' I exclaimed.

'It has to be. It's going to be made in one piece. Wheel onto it and we can see if it's big enough,' he suggested.

Although my Dad is an academic, he is very practical, with valuable skills learnt from his days growing up on a dairy farm near Camperdown in the Victorian Western District. With a few adjustments we got the depth and size of the sink just right so I could get my wheelchair under it without my feet hitting the wall at the rear.

My parents had pretty much come to terms with my situation, and their daily life was relatively normal—that is, until it all changed when I went home. They kept me informed with what was going on but didn't burden me with things like battling with the Transport Accident Commission (TAC), an insurance company, to work out the arrangements for house modifications.

Although dealing with the TAC can be frustrating at times, I am one of the lucky ones and feel very fortunate. They provide me with wheelchairs, equipment and carer support ('support worker' is the preferred term nowadays, but I will use the term 'carer' in this book) for the rest of my life. Others without insurance got very little in the way of equipment and carer support. It doesn't seem fair that a country so rich gives so little to those who really need it, where a little support can make a real difference to the quality of people's lives. However, almost three decades after my accident, the National Disability Insurance Scheme was eventually set up, and although the jury is still out at the time of writing, we all hope that long-term it will provide the necessary ongoing support to people with disabilities, enabling all to have equality, choice and fulfilling lives.

Midway through rehab my daily program had become my job, as if I was going to work each day. I wasn't sick or broken anymore; my sole focus was relearning everyday tasks. I hoped that with the passage of time I could reclaim a little of the freedom and independence I'd had before my accident. Mum had been coming daily, and on one visit I said, 'You don't need to come in every day.'

Mum may have been taken aback but didn't show it and said, 'OK, David, if that's what you want,' then started coming in every second day. Mum said she didn't see it as a rejection, but as a positive development—that I was improving and needing my independence.

I still had a long way to go and a lot of work to do to get myself as functional as possible before I went home. This gave me goals to focus on and helped keep my emotional state fairly level by not dwelling on the things I couldn't control, or the unknown. There had only been a couple of brief but overpowering moments where I felt completely doomed, but I tended to get over them quickly with the release of my mental pressure valve, as occurred on my first night in Ward 17. From memory, there was only one other time, midway through rehab, where I felt my circumstances escalating beyond my control and found myself struggling to cope with my reality.

I was at OT, again torturing myself trying to lift the small blocks off the nails, a task I was finally getting better at, when suddenly an overwhelming sense of grief came over me. It was like having a tight blanket pulled around my body with a plastic bag over my head that I couldn't pull off. As I toiled with the blocks, I struggled to hold back the tears. 'Don't bloody lose it, Dave!' I whispered to myself, but it was so overpowering I just couldn't stop the build-up of intense emotion.

I guess for that moment I stopped focusing on my immediate goals and let my thoughts wander, glimpsing the future. Even after all the months of work I had put in, a sense of any tangible progress still eluded me, and my view into the future was murky, as if someone had sandpapered a glass window and applied Vaseline.

At the time, Christine noticed that I wasn't right. 'Do you want to go back to the ward, Dave?' she said. I nodded, and she grabbed the back of my chair and wheeled me outside to wait for Hans to take me back up.

The suffocating weight only lasted a day, but it brought home to me that I couldn't see what my life was going to be beyond the walls of Ward 17.

Initially my small achievements—feeding myself or picking up a cup to drink some water, pushing my wheelchair on flat ground—fuelled my hope and gave me a sense of achievement and progress. But the periods of stagnation I was experiencing slowly ate away at the remnants of my will, like rust devouring the hull of a beached ship. Even with all the OT, physio and gym work, I didn't feel as though I was getting anywhere.

There was the frustration of learning to dress: my top half was a little difficult, but putting on tracksuit pants was near impossible. I had to sit in the middle of the bed, precariously balancing myself like a drunk Humpty Dumpty, while trying to lift one leg that had somehow changed its molecular structure to lead, then attempting to thread the tracksuit pant leg over my foot and then doing the same for the other one. If I managed to do that, I then had to somehow pull the pants up and over my bum, which was near impossible. And having a tiny nugget of poo occasionally pop out onto the bed from all the pressure put on my tummy from leaning forward, added a level of embarrassment to the frustration.

The simple task of making a cup of tea became a long and complex endeavour, requiring me to improvise, to get the job done. The microwave became my friend to heat the water in a cup instead of the kettle that I couldn't use.

Although my balance had improved somewhat and I didn't face-plant every time, transferring from the wheelchair to the bench was about as possible as holding my breath for ten minutes. This was my ticket to independence, but I just didn't have the strength or function to drag my heavy paralysed body forward in the wheelchair and lift myself across. Even if I had managed to get across, lifting my legs was another Everest to climb.

But one day in physio, I eventually saw a glimmer of hope that made the future look a little clearer. I had been practising rolling myself over from my stomach onto my back and then lifting myself up into a sitting position for months, with little success. I had mastered rolling from my stomach onto my back by propping myself up on my elbows, then twisting my torso around with my limp body following like a wound-up elastic band uncoiling. But the final and most important move that eluded me was being able to lift myself up from my elbows to a sitting position. A few other people around my level of disability had working triceps, making it relatively easy.

I didn't, which made it very difficult. Tracey demonstrated the techniques: it looked easy but it didn't work for me. And let's face it, she had full function.

As I lay on my back propped up by my elbows, feeling exhausted after trying endlessly, I suddenly had a different idea. Running a new technique through my mind, I thought: *OK, if I swing my right arm around to the back of me and lock it straight, then if I lean over, putting all my weight on my right arm and balancing momentarily, then swing my left arm around to the back, with both arms behind I could then shuffle my hands up the mat, slowly sitting myself up!* With the idea clear in my mind, I gave it a go. *Shit!* I thought as I suddenly sat up, like Dracula in his coffin.

'Trace, did you see that?' I blurted excitedly.

'See what, David?' she said a little vaguely as she was concentrating on another patient.

'Watch!' I said, dropping to my elbows, and hoping it wasn't a fluke, I did it again.

'Wow, Dave, show me again!'

I did it again, and Tracey, giggling with excitement, came over and gave me a hug.

I couldn't stop myself from doing it again and again until I was spent. I was so damn happy. After all the months of trying and trying, my efforts had finally paid off.

By sticking at these little goals, persevering even when I couldn't see progress, I could eventually achieve many of my goals. These small occasional wins kept me emotionally sane and sustained my hope for a future and for getting home.

16

DAY VISITS

Early in the new year of 1989, I began taking day visits home to start getting used to my old environment, edging my way back to where my life used to be.

Dad drove the old HJ Premier into the garage and Mum came out to help him lift me out of the car. 'Welcome home, David,' Mum said and gave me a hug and kiss.

'We'll go around the back, David, there are fewer steps there,' said Dad, pushing me around to the gate as the house hadn't yet been modified for wheelchair access.

'Back my chair up to the first step, lean me back and then lift,' I said, to make sure they understood so I didn't face-plant the concrete. With Dad on the back and Mum the front, they dragged me up the four steps to get me into the living room.

'Welcome, David,' said Dad, patting me on the shoulder then pushing my wheelchair into the centre of the room.

It felt like I had come back from a very long holiday: the house was the same as I remembered, the smell of Mum's garlic potatoes in the oven made my mouth water, my sister's shoes were still lying on the floor with the pile of newspapers, and the kitchen table was where it should be. It was as if nothing had changed. I'm not sure what I was expecting, but it seemed so very normal. 'Let us know if you need anything,' said Dad and went off to prepare the BBQ while Mum went back to finish in the kitchen.

Taking my first push inside on the carpet was surprisingly hard—something I'd have to work on—but once on the parquetry in the living area I felt much freer, able to manoeuvre easily. Rolling around the floor inspecting the bookshelf and kitchen, an urge drew me towards my bedroom, the last place I had been on the night of my accident. I felt compelled to see it.

The hallway was dark and narrow, and my wheel hit the door on the way through, bouncing off the rubber doorstop and jamming my fingers against the push rim in retaliation. My bedroom door was open, but it was a tight turn, and I needed to do a five-point manoeuvre to get my wheelchair in, with only a few scrapes of paint off the door and architrave.

I couldn't get all the way in because the gap between the bed and my wardrobe was too narrow. The familiarity of my room seemed strange. It was as I had left it, albeit a little neater: the pine desk under the window with multi-coloured curtains, a remnant of the '70s; my pine bed unusually made up on the opposite wall. Adjacent to the bed was a free-standing wardrobe with my mirror on the side; I couldn't see my reflection as I was now too short. It felt surreal. I sat absorbing the moment, thinking over what I had done on the last night I was in there on 10 July, the year before. I pictured myself walking in, grabbing the keys off my desk in the dark, then walking out down the hall, totally unaware that in a few minutes this one decision would change my life and my family forever. I breathed in deeply, and with a long exhale, I muttered to myself, 'You're a fucking idiot!' as a feeling of disappointment washed over me.

My first day visit was a big occasion. My parents had arranged for friends to come over for lunch as an early welcome home. Dad worked the BBQ and set up the outside area while Mum prepared everything else.

It was a beautiful, warm sunny day—the type of day that makes you feel good. 'Where do you want to sit?' Dad asked me.

'Over there,' I said, pointing with my fist, as he pushed me to a good spot under the shady silver birch tree in the backyard on the grass.

I was looking forward to seeing many of my friends outside the hospital environment, but I also felt a slight apprehension. I guess a part of me wanted everything to be the way it was; then there was another part that knew nothing was the way it had been. I was on a road untravelled.

As I watched Dad prepare the BBQ, Robyn, Becky, Suzie and a few others trickled through the side gate.

'Hi Dave,' Robyn yelled out with a huge smile, the three of them giving me kisses and hugs. 'You're looking good,' Robyn added cheekily.

Becky held my hand and said, 'It's great to see you, Dave, we miss you. We can't wait for you to come home.'

Each person waited their turn to approach me, as if I was some sort of royalty, which was weird, but it was wonderful to have time with each one of my friends.

Some of my friends, whom I hadn't seen for some time, were a little awkward with me; they weren't about to give me a kiss or hug, and were a little unsure as to how to shake my hand.

'Grab it like you'd shake a hand,' I said to Johnny as I thrust my hand out; he grabbed it and I slid my fingers around his. 'Good to see ya, mate,' I said.

'You're looking really good!' was the usual comment from most; I guess I was looking much better than a few months ago.

Hearing about each person's life was far more exciting than an account of my days in rehab but, to be honest, I felt a little jealous as they talked about going out and the things they got up to. I missed being with them, having fun, and I missed the normal everyday life of even going to work. I couldn't wait to get back home, still magically thinking I'd pick up where I had left off.

In the end, my apprehension about the day visit was misguided, and seeing everyone at home made me feel a little more 'me'. And my friends' initial discomfort dissipated when they realised, I was still the Dave they knew.

My day visit finished in the late afternoon when Dad drove me back to the Austin before the afternoon staff finished, in order to put me into bed.

Over the coming months I came home more often, and even stayed overnight near the end of rehab. Without the modifications at home, I couldn't go anywhere and relied on my family to help me with everything, which made going back to the Austin a little more appealing as everything was set up for me. Although I felt a little emptiness on the drive back after a brief but rejuvenating taste of being home, it gave me purpose and the motivation to work hard and learn what I needed to get back to my life.

17

GOODBYE 17

The closer I got to the end of rehab, the more my thoughts drifted to imagining what I might be able to do for a job. Work was a big part of my life and who I was. Without it, a part of my identity was missing. Dad wrote a letter to the apprenticeship board on my behalf, explaining my predicament, and they granted me the qualification as I'd only had a couple of months to go before completing my carpentry apprenticeship.

It was a nice gesture, but I was pretty sure carpentry as I knew it was out of the question. I had no idea what else I would be capable of doing. So far, I had never met or heard of anyone with quadriplegia and with my level of function who had a 'proper' job. The only person outside of rehab that I met close to my level of function was Jim with C6/7 quadriplegia; he was functionally more able than I was and visited the ward each week to chat with the patients. He was middle-aged, a very amiable guy always up for a chat, but as far as I knew he didn't work.

Was this going to be my life? I wondered. *Visiting patients to pass the time?* The only other quads I had heard of who did anything were the more able ones like Mick, or 'Super Quad' as he was known to many of us. The legend went that he could transfer from the floor, back into his wheelchair—a feat usually reserved for the paras.

Early in my rehab I asked a doctor, 'What will I be able to do?'

'With your level, you'll be able to push a wheelchair along flat ground. And I hear they're getting some quads driving again too.' He didn't mention work. Well, I could now wheel along flat ground, and I had recently attempted driving, so was this it? Was this the limit of my six percent?

Without some degree of insight into what my life could be like, what I might be capable of, or even what my potential was, I had no direction.

By March 1989, I had been in hospital for almost nine months and, like many of the patients, I couldn't wait to leave; we were chomping at the bit to move forward in our lives. But I had hoped that I would be more independent than I was. It wasn't from a lack of will or effort: six percent only went so far—or so it seemed.

Each day I did as much as I could: showering and drying my top half, unsuccessfully coordinating a sponge on a long handle to wash my bum and legs, needing the nurses to do my lower half, where I couldn't reach.

After months of swearing and frustration balancing on the bed in the OT department, falling over and hitting my head on the wall so many times I'd lost count, my meagre reward was limited to getting the tracksuit pants up to my hips and dressing my top half with a T-shirt and jumper. At least it was something.

I still couldn't transfer independently, which was my biggest disappointment. I needed help lifting my legs, but even with the bed height adjusted level with the wheelchair seat, and with the nurse or orderly in front holding my chair ready to assist, I'd strain with my spindly arms nudging my bum slowly across the slide-board, crossing the gap between the bed and wheelchair. With one last wriggle, my bum would slide into the seat but crookedly, requiring help to straighten my hips, untwist my tracksuit pants and adjust my legs.

Although I couldn't do the bigger things like my bowels, dressing or transferring independently, the many small tasks that I had relearnt and mastered through practice were great achievements for me. Whether it was feeding myself, picking up a cup, using a lighter, putting on a jumper, brushing my teeth or making a cup of coffee, I felt empowered being able to do these things without help: it gave me a sense of independence.

The gentle incline from the dining room to the main building remained my nemesis. The modest two-metre-long incline had eluded me for the last six months, the tiny bump at the top beating me every time. *Maybe the doctor was right. Maybe I am only capable of pushing a wheelchair on flat ground*, I thought. On the second-last week, as with all weeks, I tried again. As I pumped my 'chicken' arms on the run up, pushing with all my strength to gain as much speed as possible (a slow roll in my case), the chair glided up the bottom section. With my speed quickly dropping off to a standstill as I reached the top, I desperately held the wheels to avoid rolling back, my muscles twitching from the strain. Leaning forward to get a little more leverage, 'Push, push, push,' I spat to myself. With my last burst of reserve energy, the front wheels went over the tiny bump at the top, then miraculously, as if an invisible force gave me a slight nudge, the rear followed. I had done it!

I may not have been as independent as I'd hoped, but I had conquered another small Everest that had kept beating me, until now. This achievement meant a lot to me. These small things added up to something larger over time, building a little more belief and confidence in myself.

The lightweight wheelchair for my homecoming had been ordered but would take a few months to be made as it was custom-built to my size. The question of having an electric or power chair, as they're now called, came up. With my level of disability, I was on the cusp of needing one. I could wheel my manual chair over flat surfaces and now slight inclines, but for anything else I usually needed someone to push me. Having a power chair would provide limitless mobility independence and enable me to go almost anywhere.

I could see the advantages, they were obvious, but I didn't want to be in one. The power chairs in 1989 weren't that, well, sporty, and wouldn't have looked out of place in a pioneer museum. To be brutally honest, I didn't want to look so… disabled. I didn't want to be one of 'those' you see in the street whizzing past, with people quickly turning away just in case they made eye contact. These weren't rational thoughts, I knew. But they were my insecurities about how people would see and judge me.

I think it also came down to how I saw myself, my identity, early on. I may have had an obvious physical disability, but I didn't feel disabled; I still felt the same as I did before. In my mind, I was still the same six-foot-three, twenty-year-old bloke. Only when I looked in a mirror did I see a different person, someone familiar, but it wasn't me. I still wanted to be attractive to girls, I still wanted to be the man I saw myself as. I suppose I wanted to hold on to as much of me as possible.

But putting all my fears and insecurities aside, my main and most important reason was that I knew if I got into a power chair, I wouldn't get out of it. It would be too easy to stay in, and I would eventually lose any strength or fitness I had, finding it so much harder to perform the basic living skills that I had struggled for so long to relearn. It took a huge amount of time and effort to train and build up my muscles to do things they weren't designed for, and what progress I had made would have been quickly lost. Anything physical would become too hard, destroying my motivation, and it would prevent me from doing as much as possible, or ever striving to reach my true potential.

Tracey said, 'Use it for going outside the house and get in your manual chair indoors.' But I knew it was a very slippery slope.

I was only at the start of my new life using a wheelchair, and I didn't know where I would end up or who I would become. But the one thing I knew was that I had to see what I was capable of, what I could achieve and how far I could push myself with six percent functionality. And I wouldn't be able to do that if I took the easier road.

I wasn't going home straight away. The plan was for me to move into the Austin's self-contained units across the road for a few weeks, to get used to living on my own but with the support of the hospital close by.

'Let's get you ready, David,' said the nurse. All my memories, doubts, disappointments and successes in my nine-month life at the Austin were packed into two white reinforced paper bags sitting on the floor, waiting for two orderlies to arrive and take them and me to the unit across the road.

A lifetime ago, I'd arrived as a six-foot-three bulletproof nineteen-year-old, feeling the despair of losing everything that made me who I was. I had relearnt how to feed myself, brush my teeth and hair, dress my top half; I could push up a slight incline, and began to understand what quadriplegia was, although living with it would be another challenge to come. The unknown was now a little less scary; I was stronger and more equipped for what life could throw at me.

I was now ready to pick up my dignity that I had left at the door.

18

TRANSITION

The units were comfortable but fairly basic: two large bedrooms, a spacious wheelchair-accessible bathroom, a kitchen with lowered benches and a sink I could get under—not to wash dishes but to get a drink from the tap—and cane furniture with '80s patchy pastel colours throughout, the ones you see in motels that hide vomit stains.

Ken, my one and only new carer whom Thea had advertised for over the last month and was then trained up at the Austin, came in the morning to get me up. He was six feet tall with dark, unkempt hair, had a gut that dropped out from the bottom of his T-shirt like a small pillow and rode a motorbike.

As I couldn't transfer out of bed into a wheelchair, Ken would position me on the side of the bed. I would wrap my arms around his neck and he'd grab me under my bum, standing me up and lifting me onto the commode for showering or the wheelchair to get going for the day.

My morning routine was planned out. I'd get up for toileting every second day, shower, get dressed, breakfast, then off to the Austin for gym, physio and OT. It was a lot different from the production line in Ward 17. I was in charge of me now; I had to make the decisions without the advice of the nurses.

Was my bum too red? Should I stay off it until it faded? What seemed simple before now fuelled doubt as to whether I was making the right decision. I could ask the staff when I went back, but when I went home it would all be up to me. I had seen patients come back after only a short period at home with pressure sores, burns or really bad bladder infections. I didn't want to be one of them.

At the end of my day at the Austin, I'd have to find an orderly with some spare time to push me back over the bridge to the unit. Then I'd wait, passing the time by watching TV, for the designated night person to arrive. I couldn't be alone at night in case I needed help, so my sisters Madeleine, EJ and Kathryn stayed on occasion, as well as some friends, including my good mate Dave, and Janine the nurse I had become good friends with. It was odd having them there, as I had never had to rely on them in this way before, but after the nine months of dramatic changes in my life, I had become more accustomed to the unexpected.

As well as it being new for me, it was also new to my family and friends, getting to know what I could do or needed a hand with. Unknowingly, I had become accustomed to, and taken for granted, the staff at the Austin knowing everything about my care and how to assist me. This was my first taste of having to ask for help when I needed it, which I hated doing, and then explaining how to do it. For someone who hadn't seen a leg-bag before, for instance, or knew how to empty it, it could be a little bewildering.

Parking myself in front of the toilet, I'd have to instruct the person, 'OK, can you lift my foot up and put it in the toilet, please.'

'What, in the actual toilet?'

'Yeah, in the bowl,' I added to be a little more precise, as they lifted it in.

'You don't need to hold it. Just let my leg go, so it rests on the edge.'

'Like this?'

'Yep.'

'Now, pull the tube out from under the tracksuit bottom,' I'd say, giving them a minute to fumble around and find the end with a lever tap on it.

'I can't find it ...'

'It's in there, keep looking.' They would eventually find it, looking quizzically at the device.

'OK, now angle it away from my foot, but hold it with both hands so you don't piss in my shoe.' Again, they'd fumble around, trying to work out the best angle and way to hold it.

'Yep, good, now pull the lever down,' I'd say, the contents of the bag quickly draining, and hopefully not into my shoe.

I soon became aware that most people had different perceptions from me on many things: 'Cut the food into big bite-size pieces, not baby pieces. I have a big mouth!' I'd explain, being specific about what I wanted.

On one of my first nights in the unit, EJ was staying over. It was enough for me having to get used to managing my own care, let alone worrying about what to eat at night, so EJ brought over some ingredients and cooked spaghetti bolognese—one of my favourites, and easy to eat, a nice change from the hospital food or ordering takeaway.

Earlier in the day I had invited a few of the patients to come over that evening. The expected knock at the door rang out. 'Coming!' I yelled, wheeling over to the door, pushing down the handle. As I pulled the door open, it hit my chair, springing back. 'One minute,' I yelled, as I worked my chair back and forth, pulling the door with me, and realising it looked easier than it was—another task that would take some practice.

EJ had bought some beers, handing them to the thirsty travellers, and screwing off the caps for the quads. We sat around that evening until 9.30 p.m., drinking, smoking and reminiscing about past patients and our experiences, and what we looked forward to when we got home, while the radio blared in the background. As the two beers did their thing, making me very relaxed, it was the first time in so long that I felt like an adult again and a little freer, able to decide if I should have another beer. I could also enjoy the novelty of going to bed late, well past 7.30 p.m. The small taste of freedom, of having a choice and being in control of one small aspect of my life, was wonderful. Until I started to regain some freedom, I never realised how much I had missed it. I had become so accustomed to my life in Stalag 17, with the routines, the expectations and the realities of living in a hospital. The small taste of independence was giving me an appetite for more.

But one aspect of freedom eluded me: getting into bed. I was a little institutionalised by my stay at the Austin, so used to the nursing staff helping me get undressed and prepared for bed, which was normal. Then to have other people like my sisters and friends putting me to bed, seeing me naked and putting my drainage on was, to say the least, confronting and awkward.

One night my mate Dave said he'd help me into bed. At night I have to swap my day leg-bag and condom for a new condom and overnight drainage, which is a tube going into a bottle on the floor.

After Dave had helped undress my lower half, I asked him for a few minutes of privacy.

'Yeah sure, I'll wait out here. Call me when you're ready,' he said, looking directly at my face, making a conscious effort not to inadvertently gaze at my nakedness.

To put my new condom on I had to get my penis up to roll it on, then I waited a few minutes to let things settle down. 'OK, I'm ready!' I yelled to Dave in the other room.

'OK, what's next?' he asked.

'I need you to attach this tubing to the end of my condom,' I said, bashfully pulling the towel slightly away from my lap, exposing the tube at the end of the condom.

'Just plug it in like this?' he asked, grabbing the small tube with two fingers, pushing the latex tube onto the plastic connector. With each push, my condom was stretched and bent to obscure angles as he tried to force it onto the plastic connector. I held my breath, hoping to God that the movement wouldn't make my half-limp sausage awaken any further. But it defied my wishes and grew like an inflatable tube, along with my level of embarrassment with Dave stretching it against its will.

I casually put my hand on my growing member, trying to keep it down, but felt somewhat self-conscious with a body part that wouldn't behave in front of a mate. To save some dignity, I pulled the towel over my lap, although it was now propped up like a tepee.

'You need to hit it with a cold spoon, Dave,' he said, and both of us burst into laughter at the awkward situation.

As quickly as possible, I slid my body down the bed with Dave crossing my leg over and rolling me onto my side to sleep, until I was woken four hours later to be rolled onto my back.

As well as working out my care routine from hospital to the wider world, the unit helped with the psychological aspect of my transition; I gained confidence in knowing that I could manage my care without the need for the hospital support. In addition, having had most aspects of my daily life set by hospital staff for the last nine months, it helped me to get accustomed to the routine of planning and deciding what I needed to do each day and life outside of hospital. But after two weeks my time was up and I was ready to leave.

By May 1989, ten months following my accident, the extension at home was still a month away from being completed, so the TAC Rehabilitation Centre in Glen Waverley was my next home.

Compared to the Austin, the centre was a resort. It had two wards—Banksia and Acacia (they had a thing for Australian native trees) with nursing staff, self-contained units at the rear of the property, a gym, physio department, craft and wood workshops, OTs and support staff, and a huge dining room where William Angliss apprentices periodically served up an amazing three-course meal with table service as part of their assessment.

We were 'clients,' not 'patients,' and I could go to bed whenever I wanted and the night staff would help. Also, I could go out whenever I felt like it, no questions asked. As long as I got up for programs the next day, I could pretty much live my life how I wanted. This next level of freedom was fantastic.

When I arrived, there was only a handful of clients living in. Stephan from the Austin arrived not long after me; he was also waiting for his house to be modified.

Road accidents don't discriminate (although males between eighteen and twenty-five have a much higher accident rate). The other 'inmates' were a very eclectic bunch. Steve, or 'Moons,' was a biker, with a smashed ankle. He looked rough with a worn round face, curly hair and goatee, but was a gentle and considerate person. Helen was an incomplete quad, able to walk with a walking frame. A little plumpish, with an orange sweeping fringe across her round face, after a few wines she wouldn't stop talking. Margie was in her fifties, a nurse in another life, also an incomplete quad which allowed her to stand a little. She was a mothering hen, with a lot of wisdom and kind words. 'God damn my fook'n spine!' was Paul's favourite quote, another incomplete quad who could walk quite well except for when he got 'plastered,' which was often.

Stephan and I were the only 'real deal' quads.

We spent some nights in the self-contained units partying until the early hours of the morning. Usually the 'walkers' and the security guards then had to push the wheelchair users back up the hill for a few hours' sleep before program.

Between the many hours of boredom, my days were again spent at the gym and physio, working hard to get my muscles strong so I could do as much as possible.

I soon discovered a wood lathe in the workshop run by the carpenter, Paul. I had done wood-turning in Year Nine and I loved it. Paul was passionate about getting all clients working with wood. When I spoke to him about using the lathe, he said, 'Leave it to me, I'll see what I can do.' Two days later, he had built me a ramped platform to raise my wheelchair to the same height as the lathe. My only problem, apart from falling into the machine and getting ripped to bits by the high-speed rotating machinery (which was solved by a seat belt around my chest), was holding the chisels used to cut the wood away as it rotated. The craft teacher next door came to the rescue and made me some gloves that wrapped around my wrist, pulling my fingers in, so I could grip the chisel.

It might not have been building houses, but I loved being able to work with wood and do something I used to do. I spent a lot of my time in the woodwork shop making rolling pins and then more rolling pins. Guess what people got for Christmas that year!

Although I couldn't wait to get home, it was fortunate the extension was delayed another month until June. Ken, my carer, had a motorbike accident not long after I had arrived at the centre, which meant I had to replace him quickly before I went home.

I had no idea what I was doing trying to find carers. It was so new to me: no one told me how to do it, what to look for, or how to avoid the crazies. 'Put an ad in the local paper and see who responds,' was all I was told. To say it was a little daunting was an understatement.

Care work is very personal, and you have to let go of your inhibitions to a degree and see it as part of a normal everyday life. For me it's a part of life that has to be done, and over time you get used to it, sort of. Although, no matter how many years pass, having a new carer see me naked and do my care for the first time is always a little uncomfortable. However, in my first year of leaving hospital it was much more confronting, especially being so new to the game.

Following the initial phone conversation with the prospective carer to get a sense of what he or she was like and if they had any experience, I'd then meet them face to face. More often than not, whoever showed up usually got the job, as there was rarely anyone else to choose from. Although I had little idea of what I should be looking for, my intuition was switched on enough to filter some of the dodgy ones.

'So, why do you do care work?' I asked the potential carer.

'Oh, I love helping people,' she said.

Good start, I thought, until her next breath.

'I feel so sorry for you, and I would like to help you,' she said, her two kids running around screaming behind me.

Fuck! was my initial thought as my stomach tightened like shrink wrap. 'I'll be in touch!'

The last thing I wanted was someone feeling sorry for me. I wanted people who would treat me like anybody else and enable me by assisting me with the things I couldn't do or had trouble doing, and not treat me as if there was something seriously wrong with me.

Over the years of interviewing many carers and having them work for me, I have come to rely on my intuition more than anything else. The job isn't hard physically: the hardest part is remembering all the steps in the process, and these skills can be learnt, so experience isn't always necessary. Some of my best carers have had no prior experience which, in a way, is an advantage as it gives me a blank slate to train them how I want. The most important thing is whether I like them and of course that they like me, since we will be spending a lot of time together.

The first meeting is like a first date: within the first few minutes

I can usually tell if we will get along by the way they react to me and how comfortable and open they are. I like to chat with them about what they like to do, their interests, family, general things, to get an idea of who they are. Then I hit them with all the gory details about the role to see their reaction. 'So how would you feel about sticking your finger up my bum to make me crap?' I ask. If they don't flinch or turn white with a nervous bead of sweat on their brow, I'm pretty confident they'll be fine, or at least get to the next step: training.

The training is where I find out whether my intuition was right. Apart from the initial run-through on my morning routine in the interview, training is all about hands-on experience. Initially, a new carer does an observation shift to watch how it's done by an experienced carer, usually followed by two or more shadow shifts where the new carer does everything with an experienced carer providing direction. Carers with some experience usually pick up the routine fairly quickly, only requiring me to give a little guidance initially, before getting up to speed.

Most take a month to become proficient in the role, but with some it can be more demanding, taking up to a couple of months of me micromanaging them, day after day, before they are suitably competent. It's the small things I need to remind them about over and over: what the next step is or how to do it, and trying to get them to work a little faster which, over a long period of time, can become very tiring and frustrating. Everybody learns at different speeds, and because I accept that we are all different with different abilities, I make allowances. Nevertheless, it is mentally draining as I am working from the moment I wake until they leave four or five hours later, so the quicker they get up to speed, the quicker I can leave them on their own and I can start my day.

The job of a carer is completely underrated: they make a significant, positive difference to a person's life. It's not your usual job; more than anything reliability is paramount, requiring someone who is committed. If the carer is late in the morning then I may not get to an appointment, or if they don't show, I could end up in bed all day. It's not the type of job where you can pull a sicky if you don't feel like going to work. Fortunately though, through good selection and some luck, most people I have taken on have been very reliable, even coming in while sick if no one else was available. However, this level of reliability has diminished in later years, particularly with some of the younger and more transient carers.

To be able to manage different carers coming in during the week, my mornings are a set routine. The same systems and processes have to be followed each day for consistency, because if they aren't, tasks get forgotten, aren't done properly or time is wasted. One of my pet hates, apart from carers being late, is having my clothes put into the wrong drawers. It might only be a small thing to most people, but when I'm pressed and need to be somewhere on time, having the carer spend ten minutes going through every draw to find the T-shirt I want to wear is very annoying.

There has only been one time when a prospective carer didn't come back after the first training session, realising it wasn't for her. I can't remember her name, but she was around nineteen, a very sweet and kind person, with a shiny view of the world. It was her first job since completing Year Twelve, and she was considering starting a nursing degree; she thought doing some care work would be great experience.

The first day when she had to do the actual hands-on stuff, she went quite well: inserting the suppositories, then helping me transfer onto the commode to go to the toilet. As I sat on the commode over the toilet, whacking my stomach to get the contents moving with the help of coffee and a cigarette, with the intense heat lamps radiating down, it was a very hot and smelly environment for the average person to deal with.

'OK, I need some stim, thanks!' I said to the girl, nearing the end of my poo. Being her first time, she methodically and carefully slid on the plastic gloves. I couldn't help but notice that she was sweating a little, and I put it down to the warmth in the bathroom. Squatting next to the commode, she slid her hand under. A few seconds later she grunted, then gave a reactive gasp followed by a deep breath, 'Arrg, arrrg' as she gagged, her body twitching. Wobbling for a moment, she suddenly pulled her hand out with a horrified look on her face, not allowing the chocolatey glove to come near her, then ripped it off into the bin and ran out to get some air.

I couldn't help but laugh. I could appreciate that with the heat, a stench like a rotting corpse, the unfamiliarity of sticking her finger up another person's bum, and only being able to hold her breath for so long, it was all a little too much for her. She'd tried her best but decided not to come back the next time.

The tasks I need a carer to perform also determines what I look for in a person. If I were to go to a pub or shopping for clothes, I would prefer not to have someone who reminds me of my mum. But apart from age in certain circumstances, I look for varying skills and aptitudes. I can then match up what people are good at with a specific task. So, someone who can iron usually gets the ironing job rather than someone who isn't good at it or despises it. Or if I need to fix my wheelchair, I will get a person who has some mechanical aptitude and knows which way to hold a spanner. For some, undoing a bolt is as difficult to get their head around as quantum physics. This also goes for doing general maintenance on a car, such as putting water into a radiator.

Carmal was a new carer I employed some years after I had left the hospital and it was her first day working for me. 'My radiator needs some water. I'll come out and show you where to fill it,' I said.

'I'll be right, I have the same car, I know where it goes,' she said and walked off confidently to do it.

Ten minutes later she came back. 'All done!'

'Ah, great! You tightened the cap on top of the radiator where you put the water in, didn't you?' I asked, wanting to make sure it wouldn't leak when I was driving. Her face suddenly went pale, eyes expanding to the size of saucers. I knew by the look: she had just realised that she had stuffed up, big time.

'You didn't put it in the power-steering fluid reservoir, did you?' I asked, although the inlets were nowhere near each other, with totally different caps.

'God! I think I did!' she said, shaking, then running out to check.

My power-steering was never the same, but Carmal did end up working for me for over ten years, and never made that mistake again.

I've predominantly had women on my program for a few reasons. Firstly, there are far more in the industry than males, providing greater choice, but also, in my experience, women are better in the role; and when a woman has a family, she tends to be well organised, with initiative and good skills that suit the personal-care side of the role.

Further, I feel more comfortable having a woman assisting me with my care. It all comes down to a purely personal choice about who you are comfortable with, and each person will likely have a different view on what works best for them.

However, later in my life when I got into more adventurous activities such as camping, I purposefully sought specific male carers for the 'blokey' company but also for their added strength and practical abilities in doing stuff such as lighting fires, setting up camp, fixing mechanical things, lifting me back in my wheelchair or digging out a bogged car. They were generally a better fit.

Having said that, I have had a few women who would put most men to shame with their capabilities. Karen was one of those women. She was a country girl from Horsham, medium height and slim, but very strong for her size, with short mousy-brown hair, and if it was over twenty degrees she wore shorts and a singlet. Karen was one of those people who was super easy and could do virtually anything, from my personal care to rescuing wild animals to digging a car out of a bog or driving her wedding guests back home in a bus, never thinking twice about helping out. One of the first times I went snow-skiing, halfway up the mountain we had to put chains on the car. As soon as the car stopped, she was out in the freezing-cold snow and wind, working out how to fit the chains while two blokes sat in the back of the car, needing a prompt to get out and help.

A drawback to having carers is that my life is now an open book, with little privacy regarding what I am doing. This is inevitable no matter how hard I try to keep my life separate because they are in it with me every day, in all my good, bad and frustrated moods.

With each carer I have a different relationship, as we all do with the many people in our lives. With some, the relationship is more professional: they come and do their job and go; with others, when there is a connection between us, I get to see parts of their lives, families, friends, secrets and, at times, talk about very personal things. With some I have become great friends, and we have stayed friends even after they have moved on from caring. With a couple I have fallen in lust or love and had deeper relationships. Carers come into my life, I open up to them, accept them, then most move on months or years later. It is emotionally tiring to invest myself in these revolving relationships time and time again, but without them it would be impossible for me to live the life I want.

Having carers gave me choice and enabled me to get up in the morning without having to rely on my family. But coming to terms with having someone help me every single day, week after week, for the rest of my life, was overwhelming, and at times I felt frustrated and morose over the loss of my independence.

As soon as I was woken by the 'Knock, knock!', my day started. It took a few moments for my brain to register and tell my mouth to say something. Through my grogginess I moaned, 'Yeah, come in!' as the door to my room rattled and slid open.

'Morning, David!' the carer greeted me enthusiastically.

'Morning,' I said in a forced mumble, trying to sound happy.

God, I wish I could stay in bed, was my only thought. The flash of the bright fluorescent lights blinding me, I flopped my arm over my eyes until they adjusted.

Being half-asleep and having to fully exert myself physically and mentally while trying to wake up and give instructions first thing in the morning, without being grumpy, was a challenge at times—at least until I was under the shower and had time to wake up.

Having to decide a day or more in advance what time I wanted to get up in the morning so the carer knew what time to arrive added to my frustrations because it took some choice, spontaneity and freedom from my life. If I did want to sleep in after the carer arrived, especially after a late night, it wasn't always possible if the carer had to leave by a set time.

But also, having someone around me every single day, let alone having to give instructions, when all I wanted was my own space and not to have to deal with another person, felt suffocating at times. I couldn't escape. Some days, when I felt flat or I didn't have the energy to interact, I'd get up in silence, only giving the necessary instructions to the carer so I could find some solace by withdrawing into my mind.

In that state, interacting felt like a huge effort which occasionally triggered my impatience when my mental resources were low. 'No, spread the butter all the way to the edge. No, no, let it melt before the Vegemite goes on,' I'd bark, immediately feeling guilty for being grumpy, as I knew they were doing their best to help me. It wasn't anything the carer did, it was just that without relief, small inconsequential things became bigger frustrations. *I wish I could do it myself!* I'd think many times over, reflecting on my previous life when I could do most things so easily.

Trying to get some solitude in my space was difficult, with intermittent interruptions and the lack of privacy. I found it impossible to fully relax until the carer was gone. There was no time I could crawl into my cave and get away from my world of constant care; it was there when I awoke each day, and I couldn't live without it.

By the time I was to leave the TAC Rehabilitation Centre in Glen Waverley, I had found two great carers, Julie and Frances.

It was only by luck that I met Frances, as the woman I'd initially hired following Ken's departure decided to work elsewhere. Fortunately, she didn't leave me high and dry and found Frances, who was one of her colleagues in a nursing home.

Frances was in her fifties, with grey permed hair which looked natural. She wore floral dresses or blouses with blue slacks and orthopaedic shoes, reminding me of my nana. She was from Dunedin in New Zealand and had recently come to Australia after her kids moved over. Frances was a little different, which I put down to being from Dunedin. We rarely had any in-depth conversations; it was more about the weather, on which she would always comment: 'Those incessant winds!'

She didn't drive, her husband dropped her off every morning no matter what time, and she was always on time. Frances was someone I could count on—except for cutting my toenails. One morning, as I lay in bed in a half doze having my toenails trimmed, whack, my foot jumped in a spasm.

'What did you do?' I asked, lifting my head from the bed to

look at my foot.

'Oh, it's nothing,' she said, as she wiped my toe with bloodied fingers.

'You've cut my bloody toe!'

'Mmm, it's just a little nick,' she said.

It was more than a nick—it was a big chunk the size of the clippers. That was the last time I got a carer to cut my toenails. Despite this incident, Frances remained with me for many years.

Frances introduced me to Julie, who was my second carer for my program before going home. We immediately hit it off, and I found her to be a breath of fresh air. I guess being an attractive, slim and bubbly twenty-five-year-old, with bright green eyes that shone from beneath her big auburn hair, the style in the late '80s, certainly helped.

She was a lovely person and our relationship developed immediately, flourishing beyond my care into a friendship. She invited me to her friends' parties on weekends. Julie would come to my home in the evening, help get me dressed (we both wore similar brown leather jackets), load me into her car and take me to the party, where I'd thoroughly enjoy myself with a few beers, and then she'd drive me back home and put me to bed.

At one party I met a gorgeous, tall, blonde girl, also a nurse. With a long time between drinks and feeling lust-struck, I ended up pashing her towards the end of the night. Although I was quite drunk, when Julie drove me home I could tell something was up.

When she came the next morning to get me up, she still didn't seem herself. 'What's wrong?' I asked.

'Was that the first girl you have been with since your accident?'

'Well, yes, pretty much,' I said, the significance of the question suddenly dawning on me.

Our close friendship was never the same after that, and I never saw the blonde nurse again.

19

HOME

I don't remember the first time I was officially at home, or the first night I spent in my new bedroom in June 1989, but I do remember being excited about getting back to my life and feeling hopeful about the future.

The new bedroom extension on the back of the family room gave me some much-needed privacy, away from the other bedrooms, and the kitchen and family room. It was spacious, enough room for a queen-size bed, bedside tables and desk, and a large tiled en suite with wheel-in shower and a huge triangular vanity, decked out with lever taps, that Dad and I had meticulously sized when I was in Ward 17.

It was my space and my home now. It felt so good to finally escape the institutional environment, although I did miss the daily interaction and friendships I had formed with the patients and staff. But I knew that everyone would eventually move on with their lives, and it was now my turn.

I had been gone for what seemed like a lifetime, but the familiarity of the house, my sisters arguing and the smell of Mum's chop-suey, made it feel like home again. One morning as I enjoyed the warmth of the sun, my curiosity urged me to wheel over to the shed in our backyard that Dad had built back in the '70s. I managed to push the two metres to the concrete stand at the door, tied open so the adopted stray cat could sleep in it at night. My footplates hit the single step into the shed, but by leaning forward I got a good view into it. It had the same musty fuel smell but looked smaller than I remembered; maybe I was just used to large spaces for the wheelchair. I had spent so much of my childhood in the shed, pulling things apart to see how they worked and attempting to fix them on the wooden bench down one side. Tins of nails and bolts and a toolbox were neatly arranged at one end, power tools and other junk on shelves. I smiled as I recalled how much fun I'd had with my mates building billy carts and fixing our bikes.

My gaze settled on a rectangular wooden box in the corner at the back of the shed. My heart sank a little when I realised it was my carpentry toolbox, my yellow-and-red-handled chisels standing upright in their spots ready to be used, my nail bag rolled up sitting in the middle of the box, just as I remembered the last day I wore it installing shelves at Sportscraft. *I'm never using those tools again*, I thought, feeling disheartened. As I sat at the doorway the memories came and went. I felt a mixture of sadness and disagreeable acceptance of the situation, as there was nothing I could do to change it.

These powerful memories would occasionally flash in my mind when I saw something familiar. Some were so strong I could almost taste, smell or feel the moment. The patch on my surfboard made me smile as I remembered the day my mate Dave and I went surfing, and he accidentally put a hole in it on the very first day I was using it.

But these memories were fleeting. I may have felt down or despondent initially, or even for a day when I couldn't get the regret out of my head, but the feelings would pass when I got busy with other things. And over time their impact would fade, like denim jeans.

It is hard to change ingrained habits and, early on, I had to catch myself at times when an unconscious thought would arise, such as *I want some food*. Then my thoughts would catch up to the reality that I couldn't get food by myself; I required help. In hospital or at the TAC Rehabilitation Centre, there were always people around to help me if I needed assistance, whether it was preparing food or with anything else I couldn't manage; but at home, if no one was around, I had to wait. If I needed to empty my leg-bag, I had to sit and wait, my anxiety increasing as each minute ticked by, hoping that my bladder wouldn't expel more fluid, turning my condom into a balloon and exploding, wetting myself. As soon as I heard the front door open, I'd urgently wheel to meet the person. 'I need to go to the dunny, can you give me a hand?' I'd blurt.

'OK, I've just got home, can you give me a minute?'

'No, I've gotta go, I'm bursting!' I'd say, not giving them time to put their bags away as I rushed to my bathroom.

'Come on, hurry up!' I'd yell.

'All right, David, I'm coming. Hold your horses, will you!'

Not having the independence to do these things for myself left me frustrated and pissed off, but my family was usually very tolerant of my demands and always helped me out.

Some things didn't change, though, and this consistency was very comforting. Mum had always been a great cook, and eating meals I enjoyed was one of the things I'd missed the most. There were other things I wished *had* changed, such as my sisters leaving their shoes, clothes or newspapers strewn around, turning the floor into a wheelchair Tough Mudder obstacle course.

If I were ever put in prison, I wouldn't need a wall to keep me in, just a small obstacle like a gutter or a hill. In a way, the house was again my temporary prison. A concrete ramp stretched through Dad's manicured garden from the back door of the family room to the front of the house under the carport. I had no chance of getting down the steep sloping driveway by myself, let alone back up: it was a natural barrier to escaping.

Initially, I spent my time at the TAC Rehab Centre as a day patient for my usual program four days a week then, over the next year, I went only when I needed something specific such as a piece of equipment.

Both my parents worked. Mum was a secondary school teacher at Syndal High teaching legal studies and accounting, and Dad had started his private psychology practice. Kathryn had recently left nursing and just started with Qantas as a flight attendant, and EJ and Madeleine were at university. Depending on the day, once the carer left I was alone until someone came home.

I had only four hours each morning allocated for carers to assist me. Most of this time was taken just getting me up, then cleaning, and placing a meat-pie in the microwave for lunch, leaving little time for anything else. I was stuck at home, my only company the TV and my best mate Zak, my dog.

There is always an upside to really buggering yourself up, especially when you are in the ICU, on death's door. If there's something you really want, this is the time to ask for it. While the pain of your accident is burning a hole in your loved ones' hearts, hit them up with your request, starting with: 'If I ever get out of here, can I have … ?' How could they refuse you?

As I lay in the ICU, I said to my parents, 'When I get out of here, can I have a dog?'

'Of course you can, David!' said Mum.

'I want a Bull Terrier or Blue Heeler,' I said, ensuring I didn't get a yappy lapdog.

Not long after I had come home, I got Zak. He was a handsome Blue Heeler: stocky, a blue-grey colour with a white tail that was a wagging light sabre in the dark. He was obsessed with chasing balls and any cat that ran. He soon learnt how to put the ball on my lap, but any delay in throwing it quickly resulted in an extremely high-pitched yelp—he got his ball thrown a lot!

Zak was a great dog: tough, but gentle and sensitive with people. He and I became great mates, and at times he would surprise me, as if he really understood my disability.

One morning Frances forgot to put a pie in the microwave for my lunch. I opened the freezer and saw a pie near the door edge; all I needed was a long stick to get it out. I wheeled to the laundry and grabbed hold of the handle of a broom with my teeth, then dragged the broom back to the kitchen. I figured that with the handle I could flick the pie out and hopefully land it on my lap.

With a flick of the broom handle, the pie sailed past me—*kathud!*—landing on the floor. Salivating with hunger as I contemplated my frozen lunch on the floor, I realised there was no way I would manage to pick it up. Another great plan took shape: *Get Zak to give me a hand.* With his fixation on chasing balls, I just had to make him think the pie was a ball.

'Zak!' I said, pointing at the pie. 'Get the ball, get the ball!' I urged.

He looked into my eyes as if confirming that he understood. Pawing the frozen block, showing immense willpower not to eat my slowly defrosting and crumbling lunch, he delicately picked up the pie and put it on my lap. Apart from the slobber and a few teeth marks it still tasted pretty good, covered in sauce.

We spent most of our time together. He followed me everywhere and when I spoke to him, he would look at me as if he understood what I was saying. He could read my emotional state: when I was frustrated or felt sad, he'd jump up, place his front paws on my lap and lick my face to tell me everything would be OK, then run off, find a ball and con me into playing.

When I got home, a part of me expected I'd pick up my life where I had left off. I was so looking forward to going out with my friends, partying, knocking around, just doing all the things I used to. Mentally, I was still hanging on to my life before my accident, and I wanted it back.

A favourite pub on a Saturday night was the Village Green Hotel to see a cover band. It was always packed, and from my level in a wheelchair it was an endless sea of bums, crotches and boobs. Having to constantly look up and yell gave me a sore neck and exhausted me from the effort to be heard over the music. This kept the conversation limited to, 'Do you want another drink?'

Sitting low made me feel like a house surrounded by skyscrapers, with the occasional, 'Oh shit, sorry mate!' as someone bumped me in the head or shoulder and dribbled beer onto me.

'I'm going up for a dance!' I yelled, sick of being bumped by hips and bums.

'Yeah, OK, we'll come up with you,' Ian said.

Manoeuvring my chair forward and avoiding feet was like trying not to step on cow dung on a farm, as I accidentally hit ankles with my footplates or my wheels got snagged on people's toes. I'd lean forward and poke the person in front to get them to let me though. 'Sorry mate!' they'd say, and shove the few people ahead out of my way, allowing me to move forward another metre, like Moses parting the Red Sea, until I eventually reached the dance floor.

'I'm going on!' I yelled, and with a lumbering push on my wheels, I rolled across the dance floor jiggling my arms and shoulders to the beat of the music in a sort of slow-running motion. When I casually made eye contact with the girls dancing in a circle, they'd move apart to let me in, probably to avoid being run over. In my mind I was Patrick Swayze in *Dirty Dancing*, having a boogie with any girl who gave me a smile.

I caught the eye of a cute brunette and she turned towards me, shaking her shoulders and hips, bent forward to my level and urged me closer. As Bryan Adams' 'Summer of '69' came on, I rolled towards her, my running motion moves clicking into high gear. Pumped with adrenalin, I tipped my wheelchair onto its rear wheels like the 'cool' paras, momentarily forgetting how much function I didn't have. The girls cheered and clapped until— 'Oh shit!'—I overbalanced and fell backwards, hitting my head, my knees thumping me in the chest, smokes, wallet and money bouncing onto the dance floor.

'Are you OK?' asked the cute brunette, leaning over me.

'Yeah, I'm fine, just tripped!' I said casually, trying to hide my embarrassment.

'Fuck, what are you doing, Dave? How do we get you up?' Ian asked.

'Grab my shoulders and get someone at the front to push the footplates down and sit me up!' I yelled over the blaring music.

One of the girls grabbed her boyfriend and directed him to help and, with Ian, they awkwardly lifted me up. I wheeled off looking a bit dishevelled.

'Ha-ha, I'll try not to do that again,' I said, making light of the scene.

'We're going to go soon, Dave.'

'The night's just starting, mate! Let's have a couple more drinks!' I insisted.

'I'm driving, so that's enough for me,' said Ian.

After being dropped off at home at 1 a.m., I pushed up the driveway and the sensor light flashed to life, illuminating the path to my room at the back of the house.

My door slid open. 'Do you want a hand, David?' Dad said.

'Yeah, that'd be good,' I said, trying not to slur, smelling of spilt beer and cigarettes.

Dad undressed my top half. I tried to act as normal as possible, but my lack of balance to keep myself upright was a dead giveaway—

it was a stretch to blame it on my quadriplegia.

'Do you want a hand, Brian?' Mum said, poking her head through the door and eyeing off my dishevelled look.

'I wish you wouldn't drink so much, David,' said Mum.

'I'm fine,' I said, not feeling up to the task of debating the point.

Leaning forward, Dad lifted my bum into bed, then my legs and undressed me. 'You're a bit wet, David.'

'Oh, am I? My conny must have leaked,' I mumbled, which explained why my leg-bag wasn't filling later in the night.

Dad grabbed my arm to sit me up so I could drag my naked body up to the bedhead. Like a spinning top losing its momentum, I overbalanced, fell back and slammed my head into the headboard; thankfully it was padded. Dad grabbed my arm again and sat me back up to have another go. With a few more pushes I made it, then had to deal with fitting a new condom and drainage on a non-reactive member as a result of the booze—nine out of ten on the difficulty scale.

Completely shagged and not feeling too good, I let my body fall backwards, my head on the pillow. Dad crossed my leg over so I could roll later in the night if I woke up, then covered me up.

'Good night, David,' he said, switching off the light.

Apart from having a hangover that felt like I'd been hit by a bus, then backed over a few times while sucking on its exhaust pipe, I woke up late the same day with my conscience unwilling to let me off the hook. I felt guilty for putting my friends and family in a situation where they ended up having to look after me instead of helping me, a situation I'm sure they would have preferred to avoid.

Also, my self-respect felt a little dented when I considered that people might think I was more disabled than I was, given my compromised balance; I wasn't filled with warm thoughts about myself. But I also cut myself some slack; drinking allowed me to escape my reality, albeit briefly. But more than anything, I think I was desperately trying to recapture a part of my life that once was, because after losing so much physically, I wasn't ready to give up everything.

However, over time I began to realise that some parts of my former life, like this one, weren't worth recapturing, and I had to move on. Getting hammered wasn't doing my health any good, especially when it stopped me peeing. This caused my bladder to overfill, which could result in kidney damage over the long term. Additionally, forgetting to empty my leg-bag, blowing off my condom and wetting myself risked damaging my skin with urine burns.

Also, it wasn't worth putting my family through my drunken ordeal when they wanted to avoid seeing me like that. And going out with my mates was no longer the same; they seemed more responsible than previously, not going crazy like they once did, and if I was a 'wee' bit inebriated, they had to be relatively capable to help me.

But my strongest incentive to refrain from heavy drinking was that it made me more disabled than I was. With impaired balance, coordination and motivation, it watered down what little independence I had, making me depend on my family and friends to help me do some of the things I had worked so hard to achieve. I didn't want to be like that; I didn't want to lose some of my independence, even for a night. It just wasn't worth it, and I knew I had to leave it behind.

I know it doesn't sound pretty but, to be honest, it was necessary for me to experience what I had lost, a kind of mourning, in a way. I had to see for myself what I thought I was missing, then come to terms with the reality of my situation and make the decision to move on. Only then could I let go.

We didn't have video games or a home computer; the internet hadn't been invented and I wasn't into reading. If I wasn't going anywhere during the day, once I was up and my carer had left late morning, I was on my own to fill the rest of the day. *The Morning Show*—the highlight being the aerobics session with Cheetah and the other toned blonde girls and token guy—worked off an hour or two in the morning.

On a nice day I'd sit in the sun warming myself, my thoughts often drifting to what I would be doing at this moment in my 'first life' on a building site, then further ahead, hoping for an epiphany about what I could do now. Then Zak would bark, bringing me out of my daydream. 'OK, gimme the ball, gimme the ball,' I'd say as he reached up and put the slobbery piece of chewed rubber on my lap.

My day's highlight came at 12.30 p.m., dialling in three minutes on the microwave to heat my lunch, then scoffing the soggy, piping-hot Four'N Twenty pie with sauce. My full belly drained me of energy and with nothing on TV apart from the soapie, 'Days of Our Dreary' (as I called it) to distract me, the lethargy would set in. All I wanted to do was lie down in bed to pass the time, but I couldn't even do that. The weight of tiredness would grow heavier, as did my desperation to get a little shut-eye to help me through a few more hours. Unable to hold my head up, my eyes drooping closed, I'd grab the pillow at the top of my bed with my teeth, drag it to the edge and lean onto it for a much-needed nap. Around twenty minutes later I'd wake up groggily, with sweat on the right side of my face caused by the pain my body could feel (but I couldn't) inducing mild autonomic hyperreflexia (also known as autonomic dysreflexia which, in severe cases if left untreated, can be fatal), in which there is a sudden onset of excessively high blood pressure caused by the very uncomfortable position. Feeling a little less tired, to pass the remaining hours, I'd sometimes resort to pushing up and down the ramp in the backyard, my body and mind on autopilot. Each day blurred into the next, dragging on for what seemed an eternity.

To try and make my day a little less monotonous and give me some purpose, I decided to cook for the family once a week. My recipe of choice was a relatively easy one for me to cook and one of my favourites—chicken rogani, a dish similar to rogan josh but with capsicum and cream. But there was a catch: it required a lot of chopping.

My parents had recently remodelled the kitchen with a low triangular corner bench for my hot-water urn so I could make a cup of coffee during the day, and it was big enough for a cutting board and electric wok. In the morning, my carer measured out the spices into a small container to make it easy for me to add when cooking, and put the onions, capsicums and thawing chicken on my corner bench ready for me to prepare. Using my 'innovative' pine cutting board with a large blade knife attached with the pointy end bolted to a swivelling pin, it was effectively a small guillotine—perfect for a bit of 'Yubitsume' (cutting one's finger off) if you're a fan of the Yakuza (Japanese organised crime syndicate).

Parking myself under the bench, rolling the first capsicum into position, lining it up lengthways to the knife, I'd bring the blade down enough to hold the condemned vegetable in position. Using my left hand to steady the knife, with my right hand I'd give the handle a whack. Chomp! The blade would slice through the helpless vegetable, the quarter dropping away like the head of Marie Antoinette. Rolling the capsicum over a quarter-turn onto the new flat section, again lining it up with the length of the blade, chomp, chomp, chomp would go the other sides, methodically taking off each cheek until only the core was left. Annoyingly, the seeds would scatter all over the board with strays ending up in my crotch, where they would have to stay until I went to bed. Using my trained carpenter's eye, I'd line up the first cheek lengthways with the knife, getting it just right to cut off a one centimetre wide strip. I'd bring the knife down, giving the handle a whack. Twenty minutes later, with a few rests, the whole capsicum would be sliced into one centimetre strips. I'd then take each individual strip and cut it into one centimetre pieces, working much faster, slamming the knife down quickly like a stamping machine, making sure I didn't do a Yubitsume on myself.

Four hours later, the remaining vegetables and the chicken breasts (which behaved like a rubber boot being cut with a hammer) were diced and my task was complete.

Although the kitchen was small I'd roll around the bench with ease, leaning over, balancing on one elbow on the bench to grab the bottle of olive oil with two hands, dropping it in my lap, careful not to let it slip between my legs to the point of no return, and wheel to my work bench, positioning it close to the edge so I could grab it when I needed it. The new fridge was the upside-down type with the fridge part up top, making it easy for me to get the bottle of cream and tomato paste by licking my forefinger and thumb for added grip and wrapping my gummy fingers around the bottles. Back and forth I went, getting each item I needed, positioning them around the wok in the order I needed to use them to make it easier.

With my family soon arriving home at 6 p.m., the climax of cooking was the easy part. Plonking each ingredient into the sizzling wok, I would stir the mixture with my preferred wooden spoon wedged between my fingers. I knew it was time to give my tired arm a rest when the spoon lost traction and flicked onion, capsicum and cream onto my jumper.

I enjoyed the creative process, adding a little more or less of each ingredient to give the dish my own touch, the sweet spicy fragrance filling my nostrils and making my mouth water. I felt tremendously satisfied creating something again and being productive, especially for my family to enjoy.

My friends were at work during the day, but I was fortunate that Janine, the nurse I'd met at the Austin, who was now a good friend, would take me out driving in her little green Gemini on her days off. Some nights we'd see bands with her nursing friends, and when I was home she'd put me to bed so as not to disturb my parents and sisters who had to do it every other night.

I had also become good friends with Brigid (or Bwidgy), our favourite night nurse when I went through the TAC Rehab Centre. After her rounds she'd join us in the TV room, chatting as she knitted a jumper. Bwidgy was very laid-back, which appealed to me. In her late thirties, she had a bun spiked with what looked like spare knitting needles to hold up her grey hair. On many occasions after a few hours' sleep in the morning to recover from her nightshift, we'd go for a drive up to the Dandenong mountains or to the beach on a mission to find Victoria's best fish and chips. Following much research and increased cholesterol, we determined the best was in San Remo near Phillip Island.

Bwidgy was also good friends with the other crew when I lived at the TAC—Moons, Paul, Margie and Helen. On Bwidgy's nights off, we had quite a few entertaining evenings drinking port at her house with her husband Ian, or Chambo, as he was known. Catching up with them was always good fun and, in a way, it was also therapeutic as it gave us the opportunity to talk with people who could understand what we were experiencing. It was acceptable to bitch about your disability, to unload your frustrations and talk about what was pissing you off when you were having a lousy day or week.

A life-changing event doesn't just change you, it changes all aspects of your life.

Strangely, some of the people I thought wouldn't hang around after my accident have done so, while others I thought would, haven't. This is not a good or bad thing; it's just the way it is, for various reasons.

With most of my friends working, I rarely saw them during the day. Pete, Dave, Mick and a few others occasionally came over at night; we would sit in my room kitted out with a TV and stereo, smoking, having a few beers and talking. It was always great to see them, but I could sense that our relationships had changed.

Before my accident, our friendships were built on doing physical stuff, going out to see bands, working on our cars, surfing, snow-skiing, our jobs—things I could no longer do. Now we were sitting around talking about the 'good ole' days. I loved hearing about their lives, but my life revolved around getting up in the morning and maybe going out for an occasional drive during the day.

And when I went out with my male friends, the dynamic had changed; where once we were 'knock around' mates, now they were careful not to drink too much as they were responsible for looking after me. I guess my disability may have been a little confronting for some. It wasn't just having to manhandle me in and out of a car or push me around, but some of the more personal things, such as assistance with emptying my leg-bag. For some, I knew it was uncomfortable, so if possible I would get one of the girls to help me.

This also made me feel like a burden. I didn't like asking them to help me all the time, and this made me reluctant to initiate social arrangements. I didn't want them to feel I'd asked them because I needed their help rather than because I wanted their company. The fact was, I didn't fit into my mates' world anymore, and mine was so foreign to them. I felt jealous at times that they were living their life, the life I'd once had. I wanted my life back, but it was never going to be the same. I felt I was being left behind. Emotionally I waved goodbye as I watched many old friends disappear into the distance.

But with my female friends it was a little different. Perhaps because these relationships weren't based on physical capabilities, but on companionship and emotional connection. We'd catch up for coffee, dinner, movies or a chat. It was easier to connect with them since my accident; I could talk to them about my feelings, and they were also more accepting and comfortable with me. Fortunately, some of my close female friends have remained in my life to this day.

20

BACK BEHIND THE WHEEL

Turning eighteen meant we could go to pubs legally, but the privilege we most looked forward to was getting a licence to drive. Having a licence meant independence instead of having to rely on irregular public transport or our parents' taxi service. Also, working as a carpenter, I needed to get to the construction jobs by myself. In the first year of my apprenticeship, I had to rely on Vic, my boss, to pick me up in his old Holden HQ panel-van and was forced to listen to him singing along to 3AW's passé hits.

I couldn't wait to get my licence, and the day I got it I felt like a caged bird set free, although I was a little limited with Dad's hand-me-down Mazda 1200. I had to drive it until I had saved up enough money to buy my own car. The Mazda was a piece of junk, the best part of the car being the peeling white duco. Putting your foot down for a quick take-off at the lights left a smoke trail to rival the exhaust blast from the space shuttle launch, blanketing the car behind. And trying to stop was like Russian roulette, having to guess which way the car would pull, to left or right, as I hit the brake pedal—if the brakes worked at all. But it was free!

When I bought my first car, a poo-coloured Holden HJ Premier with a throaty V8, the added reliability and safety was like spreading my wings for full flight. My first big road trip was heading up to

Port Macquarie with Pete and Mick, where I learnt to surf. With this mobile independence, my friends and I would drive to the coast on weekends, surf all day until we were contentedly tired and starving, then feed our faces with fried dim-sims, chips and a can of Coke for the drive home. Fun times!

Two years later, I was back where I'd started: relying on my parents to drive me or getting taxis. Wheelchair-accessible vans didn't exist, only the standard taxi sedans; it was traumatic for the taxi driver who had to get me in and out of the car as I was unable to transfer myself, which only fuelled my frustration.

Given that for many taxi drivers English was a second language, it was very difficult to explain how to get this heavy, floppy six-foot-three body into the car. 'Put my legs in, now lift my hip up, slip the slide-board under my bum, lift me up and hold the chair,' I'd explain in detail, as a blank face stared back at me, with the head shaking as he tried to understand the alien gibberish from my mouth.

The shortfall in communication occasionally caused my wheelchair to shoot out and me to land on the ground, swearing my head off at the poor bewildered Asian immigrant taxi driver for purposely letting the chair go and not attempting to understand my clear and precise instructions.

'I fix you, I fix you!' he'd say, skipping around me, grabbing both my arms, trying in vain to lift an eighty-kilogram dead weight.

Over the months my frustrations increased and patience dwindled. My thoughts kept going back to my first driving experience at the Austin Hospital when I was in rehab a year earlier.

The Austin had a driving instructor, John, who would come down from Shepparton every couple of months to give some of the patients, mainly the paraplegics, a go at driving his Ford Falcon sedan using hand-controls.

As I watched what was going on in the rear carpark one afternoon, a nurse came up to me and said, 'David, do you want to have a go?' I had to think for a minute to process what she was saying. I immediately thought, *You've got to be kidding, aren't you? I have quadriplegia.* 'Ah … yeah sure, I'll have a go!' I said, a little surprised. I figured if they were silly enough to let me drive, I'd give it a crack. I couldn't do much more damage to myself anyway.

Brian and Gussy the orderlies picked me up. Brian, the tallest, was at the top holding my top half while Gussy had one hand under my bum and the other trying to thread my heavy legs under the dash; then they poured the rest of my limp body parts into the driver's seat. Securing me with the seat belt and a strap around my chest so I wouldn't fall over into John's lap, he gave me a quick rundown on how the hand-controls worked.

'See that lever there on your right?' John said, pointing to a horizontal lever above my right knee.

I put my hand on it. 'Push it down towards your knee to accelerate or push it towards the dash to brake. You OK with that, Dave?'

'Yep, no probs!' I said, pushing it down and forward to get a feel for it.

On the steering wheel was a U-shaped device that my left hand slid into so I could turn the wheel. What could go wrong?

Within the hospital grounds was a very windy road that went from Ward 17 to the bottom of the hill.

I was unable to turn the ignition key, so John leaned over and started the engine. 'OK, let's go!' he said. 'Brake on?'

'Yep, on!' I said, as he put the car into gear (it was an automatic). As I released the hand-control brake lever, the car slowly crept forward, my heart speeding up: I was driving! A little unsure as to how quick I could turn the steering wheel, I kept my hand on the brake, travelling at a walking pace.

The resistance on the steering wheel made turning difficult, and after the first two corners my arm felt like lead so I pulled over for a rest. After a short break, John insisted we get going so we proceeded around the grounds then came to the gate entrance to the hospital, where I expected we'd turn around.

'OK, let's go on the road,' he said.

'Do what?'

'You'll be right,' he said.

I was somewhat nervous but also very excited at the prospect. Taking a deep breath, throwing caution to the wind, I drove onto the not-quite-busy road. Though a bit nerve-wracking at first, it was actually easier driving in a straight line than around all the turns in the hospital, and it became more so as I grew more comfortable using the hand-controls. Thank God no cars jumped in front of me, as I doubt my reaction time would have been any good at that stage. By the time we had driven around the block and got back to the rehab building with a few rests along the way, I was exhilarated and driving began to feel familiar again.

I surprised myself that day. I hadn't known whether I'd ever be able to drive, let alone so early and in rehab. No practice, just thrown into the deep end. Sometimes, I've found, this is a good way to tackle things we are unsure of or are scared to try. If given time to think about it, we may miss the opportunity to step outside our comfort zone and achieve something we may not have thought possible. That day a new seed was sown: driving = independence.

'Fuck this shit!' I blurted as I lay on the ground at the TAC Rehab Centre following another less-than-successful transfer into a taxi after a three-hour wait for it, which really pissed me off.

'Go get the bloody receptionist!' I yelled at the bewildered taxi driver. Jane came out. 'I'll get someone to help David,' she said, walking briskly into the building to call the gym.

Within a few minutes, Tracey and Des, the gym instructors, had me off the ground and into the taxi.

It was the final straw. *I'm not going to keep doing this shit!* I promised myself on the drive home; the driver was too scared to make a sound.

Tom, my occupational therapist at the TAC, arranged some driving lessons at another rehab centre, but it didn't go well from the start.

The day of my first lesson was a scorching 35 degrees and I was overheating before I even started, unable to control my body temperature. The Magna car was small, the door opening best suited to kids, and the musty, humid draft from the air-conditioning unit that smelt like armpits made me feel even hotter.

Nothing was right: I was cramped and couldn't sit right, which made it hard to balance; the steering was heavy: when I tried to turn the wheel with my hand in a three-pronged device that resembled a robot's claw, two of the prongs bent, causing my hand to slip out. I didn't even make it out of the carpark.

By the end of the one-hour session, I had a full leg-bag of piss that I couldn't empty and was too embarrassed to ask someone. I felt totally deflated as I sat in front of an air-conditioner waiting for a taxi.

But the experience wasn't without value. I now knew that if I wanted to drive, I had to get my own car and set it up the way I needed.

Looking for a car to buy that I could drive presented some difficulties, given I couldn't test-drive it. Dad and I went to numerous car yards all over Melbourne looking at various models. Dad would get me in, and with the engine running but stationary, I worked the controls and steering to see what was easiest to use.

I finally settled on a 1985 Ford Fairmont Ghia, an upmarket model, with the lightest steering I could find, big doors to get in, and fantastic air-conditioning and heating—a must—plus electric windows.

I sent the car off to 'Dodgy Engineering' to have the same hand-control fitted as the one I'd tried at the Austin Hospital and the same steering fork that I knew I could use. I was then ready to go. This time, no instructor: just me and the car.

Home was in Glen Waverley, a leafy middle-class outer suburb of Melbourne, with only the occasional car driving down our street.

Dad finished setting me up in the car with a strap around my chest; Mum yelled from the front patio, 'Be careful, David!'

'Yes Mum,' I mumbled to myself.

To test the brakes, I pushed the hand-control lever above my knee towards the brake and the car stopped: nice and easy. To accelerate, I pushed the same lever towards my knee. Simple!

Dad got in the car for the initial run to see how I would go. Edging the car slowly down the drive, I turned left as it was much easier to turn the steering wheel in that direction, then I applied a little throttle and the car gathered more speed. I rocketed to the first corner at twenty km/hr; coordinating the brake and steering at the same time took all my concentration, while the chest strap pulled tight stopped me from falling over. I took the first corner, successfully missing the parked car, then around the second and down Chivalry Avenue.

'I've got to pull over for a rest,' I said, my arms tired and aching. They were not used to the movements and I fatigued very quickly. Dad was always pretty relaxed with these things. When I was ten or so he let me drive the old Mazda 1200—when it was in much better condition—on the quiet roads near my uncle's dairy farm in Camperdown. He would fall asleep and I'd wake him when I came to an intersection to ask which way to go, although I'm sure he had one eye open.

'That's OK, take your time,' he said. I felt almost beaten; it was so much harder than I thought it would be, and I didn't know if I would ever have enough endurance to drive on a busy road. Once I'd regained some strength in my arms, we started off again. Up, around the bend to the next corner, pulling over again for another rest. We continued in this way around the large block, all left turns, until we arrived home. I felt victorious, although damn tired.

Now that I felt confident to attempt it alone, Dad got out and I headed off. Around and around I drove, always left corners with many, many rests.

My endurance quickly grew, and the familiar circuit became bigger and bigger, encompassing right and left turns. Soon I was ready to go onto the main road with traffic. My confidence to drive returned quickly, and my skills using hand-controls eventually became second nature.

Following many hours of practice, I was confident about my driving ability, but my friends Dave, Bec and Suzie weren't so. One night we planned to go to the local cinema. 'I can drive you all, if you like?' I asked. I had no takers, so I drove by myself and met up with them in the carpark so Dave could get me out. I wasn't surprised or too disappointed, but it wasn't long before they realised I was probably a safer driver now than before my accident.

Although I couldn't get myself in or out of the car, driving was the most rewarding goal I had achieved in my first year of being home. To be able to go out on my own was so liberating. I could escape the confines of my home, my wheelchair, even for a little while; driving gave me a little more control in my life. It also gave me more independence, and a taste of the freedom I craved like a drug. And, like any addiction, I wanted more and more. My ultimate dream was to be able to get in and out of the car myself but this, like getting myself into bed at night, seemed impossible.

21

TRYING NEW THINGS

Apart from close-range blow darts, in 1990 there weren't many activities available to people with high-level quadriplegia.

I had always been into the more active sports, either for the adrenalin rush or the physical battle of contact. I had grown up playing Aussie Rules football through both primary and high schools, and played for the local club, Glen Waverley Hawks. Being the tallest, I was made ruck most of the time. I liked this position because I could move all over the field and be in the action instead of waiting for the ball to occasionally come down my end for a spurt of excitement. I also liked the contact and roughness; I felt like a gladiator going in to battle, putting my body on the line.

I considered myself fairly resilient when it came to pain: when I was ten I didn't even cry when my mate Darren threw a brick at my head by mistake, causing me to need seven stitches. I went back out to play when the doctor had finished with me, although I did have a headache. The risk of taking skin off my bum or legs when we raced our homemade billy carts just made it that much more exciting.

In 1990, two years after my accident, I gave swimming a go, but with limp legs that sank like rocks, and unable to control my body temperature in the cold water, the fun factor was equivalent to going to the dentist for a root canal. And, to be honest, it was painfully boring.

Not long after my swimming debut, a game that originated in Canada in the 1970s was going to be played for the first time at Genazano College basketball stadium and they were looking for players. It was called wheelchair rugby. It sounded rough, and I could possibly get hurt—*Where do I sign up?*

When I arrived at the stadium, wheelchairs were everywhere like ants running to honey. It looked like every quad in Melbourne with varying levels of function had dragged themselves out of winter's hibernation for the event.

Wheelchair rugby, or Murder Ball as it's called in Canada, is a game designed for people with quadriplegia. The players have impaired upper and lower body function and are given a point rating depending on their level of function. The least-able player is 0.5 with the most able at 3.5, more similar to a paraplegic, although there are varying functional ranges.

Four players from each team are on the court at any one time, with the maximum value of the team being eight points. To score, you cross a back line similar to rugby league, and players can use their wheelchair to block.

It was exciting, but we knew very little about the rules or how to play. All we had were our standard wheelchairs, no straps to hold us in and no tip bars (a bar at the back of the wheelchair to stop you flipping out backwards if you leant too far back). Such bars were unheard of then.

The eclectic bunch was split into teams. The general rules—a player can hold the ball for ten seconds, then he or she must either bounce or pass it, hopefully without falling out. To score, a player must have possession of the ball and cross the back-scoring line—between two witches' hats—with two wheels of their wheelchair.

As soon as the whistle blew, it was every man or woman for themselves—total chaos! With arms flailing, the ball ricocheted off one player to another all over the court. The faster players moved quickly down court after the ball at running pace. Chairs crunched, players lost balance falling forward or out to the side, with others rolling out of control into walls. The least-able players like myself, being a 0.5-point player, pushing flat out at walking pace, tried to catch up to the herd moving down court. Once I'd almost reached the group, back the other way they would come, passing me on the way. The only time they made contact was when they ran into me.

Broken necks weren't the problem; the issue was the chance of head injuries from repeated falls onto the floor. The ball would come screaming towards me—whack!—straight in my face, knocking me backwards with the chair tipping up, my head making a dull thud as it bounced on the hard wooden floor. Two 'uprights' ran out, lifted me back up, straightened my twisted body, then play resumed. That's the way it was. Bloody awesome! In the early games, we would all fall back many times, whacking our heads—until we got serious and installed removable tip bars.

The ball spent more time on the ground than in our hands, but it was so exciting and tremendous fun.

Four teams of four were initially established for a local competition, and our team had a coach for a while. Being the 0.5, the slowest and least-able player on the team, the coach wanted me to sit in front of the goal to slow down any opposition looking to score. Sitting there moving back and forwards eight metres along the goal line was boring and wasn't me. I needed to be 'having a go' and getting into the thick of it, like in football; I'm not a spectator.

As I sat in front of the goals, Michael, a new incomplete quad who could walk with crutches, came screaming down the court. He momentarily fumbled with the ball, taking his eyes off where he was heading. I pushed my chair over one metre in anticipation, and without looking up he ran straight into me, flying out of his chair, crumbling to the ground and losing the ball. Dumbfounded, he looked up, wondering where the hell I had come from. I got a 'turnover.' It was pretty funny, and I had a good laugh at Michael's expense.

As he picked himself up off the floor into his chair, the coach and a supporter came running over to congratulate me and gave me a piece of orange to replenish my energy for my 'heroic,' 'marathon' effort.

I knew they meant well, but I felt embarrassed by their well-meaning actions. I hadn't done anything. In that moment I felt like a disabled person, not a person with a disability. I didn't want to get credit for something that took very little effort. I felt it reduced the value of me, the person. To me, it's important to get credit only when it's deserved, when it has been earnt, whether I am in a wheelchair or not. If I had slogged my guts out and pulled off a good move, then sure. It was like being told you're 'inspirational' for just getting out of bed in the morning.

I stopped turning up.

Alison, the recreational coordinator at the TAC Rehab Centre, helped a group of us to form a disabled shooters club under Wheelchair Sports Victoria (now Disabled Sport and Recreation) in 1990.

A president was needed so Alison nominated me, not that I had any idea what I was to do. Other people undertook various roles, and the Physically Challenged Shooters Club was formed.

The Sporting Shooters Association of Australia (SSAA Vic) supported our club by providing air rifles and the use of their ten-metre indoor shooting range. Alison did some research and found that people with similar disabilities in the USA used stands with a spring that supported the rifle in the middle, but still allowed it to wobble around requiring the shooter to steady it, aim and shoot.

One of the engineers at the TAC made a couple of stands with the right tensioned spring, and with a bit of trial and error, we were shooting regularly on Tuesday nights.

We used a gas-powered air rifle over a ten-metre range with open sight. The target was the size of a twenty-cent piece, the bullseye a pinhead. Looking through the sight, the target resembled a small black dot.

Viv, Glenn and I were the regulars with a few others coming from time to time. The SSAA were very supportive and Alex, one of their members, helped us every week without fail: setting us up, loading the rifles, changing targets and giving us advice on how to shoot.

I got the hang of shooting fairly quickly. It's a disciplined sport that requires concentration for extended periods of time. Although you don't need to be super-fit, being fit helps with concentrating, relaxing and slowing down your heart rate as the thump of the heartbeat knocks you off aim—so you shoot between heartbeats.

Over the next few months I progressed quickly, shooting consistently nines and tens, with tens being the highest score. The three positions we shot were Standing, Kneeling and Prone. With Standing you could use a table without any body part resting on it, the stand supporting the rifle. Kneeling was the same but with one elbow on the table, and Prone was with both elbows on the table.

Alison had been chatting to one of the organisers of the 1991 Oceania Shooting Championships in Adelaide and I was asked if I wanted to compete.

We had competitions at the club, but this promised to be an amazing experience, considering I had never competed in anything like it before—so 'Hell, yes!' I said.

Janine came with me; I borrowed a club gun, loaded my car and drove to Adelaide with some sightseeing on the way. We arrived in Adelaide, but it being a Sunday, I had no idea where I was to go for the tournament, which was starting the next day. I hadn't been given any details and few people had mobile phones then, so I couldn't call anyone until they came into the office on Monday.

Janine and I drove all over Adelaide, finally getting directions to a basketball stadium with the ranges set up inside.

I had no idea what to expect—which probably helped me. Without any expectations, there was no pressure. I went in and just did my best. Although I had been shooting for only a few months, I was very surprised when I won gold in the 3 x 40 (Standing, Kneeling and Prone x 40 shot for each position).

I enjoyed the shooting; it was challenging, requiring strong mental and physical fitness. But my genetic makeup was geared towards pursuits that offered more excitement and physical demands. I missed the contact sport of football and the adrenalin rush of skiing and surfing. I needed more.

I had heard on the grapevine that wheelchair rugby was still going and the focus had changed, with the different levels of ability playing more specific roles. I decided it was time to have another go.

22

CROSSROAD

I struggled to come to terms with my reliance on carers—having to depend on someone to get me up every morning and put me to bed. More than that, it was the loss of choice and spontaneity: the ability to do what I wanted, when I wanted.

There were many times I was so bored or tired at home alone; I wished I could just lie down for an hour. But without someone to help me, I couldn't get myself into bed. Anything requiring assistance had to be planned in advance.

Deep inside me I hoped that somehow, some day, I might be more independent; but this was a future I could not even picture.

At home the carers got me up in the morning, but I had to rely on Mum, Dad and my sisters to help me into bed and get me undressed, which was the hardest. I felt embarrassed; I felt I had lost my manliness, my pride.

With the loss of independence came the loss of identity. Who I used to be was in another time. I considered myself to be the sum of everything I did, the markers that made me who I was—carpenter, surfer, skier; tall, strong and untouchable. I was no longer any of these things. 'David's a quadriplegic,' people would say. Was this all I was now, just a quadriplegic? Did my disability define me? Was I only 'six percent' of the person I used to be?

Even after being home for over a year, I still couldn't transfer out of my wheelchair onto a bed, and I was still working out how to get undressed on my own.

I wanted to be as independent as possible, to stretch my six percent as far as it could go. Each day I tried to do as much as I could. The skills I had learnt during rehab—washing my top half in the shower, brushing my hair, cleaning my teeth, dressing my top half, making coffee and so on—I could do easily.

When I became proficient at one task, I focused on the next goal—which could take anything from a few goes to many months of trial and error. Working out how to roll myself at night was a fairly quick process once I had figured out how to position my legs in bed and use the overhead slings on a frame above me.

The task of giving myself suppositories to activate my bowels at five in the morning before the carer arrived an hour later was a big challenge. I can say with some authority that being half asleep, trying to balance on one elbow on my side while I stuck the 'sup gun' up my bum-hole was not easy. The sup gun consists of a metal frame that wraps around the hand with a ten-centimetre hollow plastic tube in the centre to hold the suppository. The idea is to poke it up your bum and it leaves the suppository behind when it's removed. It makes your eyes water, doesn't it?

At times, simple modifications to an off-the-shelf product made it possible for me to do something where previously I couldn't. To enable me to get my leg-bag on and off my leg, loops were sewn onto the ends of the leg-bag straps that allowed me to hook the loops with my gummy fingers.

To undo a shirt or jean button, I was given a buttonhook that consisted of a wooden handle with a strap around it to hold it on my hand, with a wire loop on one end of the handle. By putting the wire loop through the buttonhole and over the button, then pulling, the button would pop through the hole. To get it undone, you just did the reverse.

The months ticked by, but ever so slowly I relearnt a few more small things, gaining a little more independence, a little more pride in myself, one small goal at a time.

I was at a party with Janine and her nursing friends when I got chatting with a guy called Phil. He had been in a chair for sixteen years and was reasonably independent, although he had more function than me.

'You won't know yourself when you can get yourself home and into bed,' he said.

I thought about it for a moment. 'I'll never be able to do that,' I replied.

It just seemed so impossible. To go from struggling with small everyday tasks to taking such a light-year-sized leap was much like trying to imagine myself climbing Mt Everest or harnessing the power of levitation. Not a hope!

When friends came over or I went out and returned late, my parents or sisters would have to get up, no matter what time, get me out of the car and put me to bed. I don't recall them ever complaining, even when it was after midnight and they had to go to work the next day.

At times, I felt guilty wanting to stay up late when I knew they wanted to go to bed. The more time passed, the greater my need for more independence. I had now worked out how to get undressed once I was on the bed, but the barrier to more independence was a four-inch gap between my chair and the bed. The gap might as well have been the Grand Canyon—I couldn't get across it.

If I could have had one wish (apart from a new spinal cord), it would have been that I could transfer myself. Just to get a fraction of independence so I didn't have to rely on my family all the time.

A tiny bit of relief from my physical imprisonment was all I wanted.

I think out of desperation, due to the frustration of having to rely on my family, I had reached a crossroads: I could either resign myself to being dependent on my family or carers to get me in and out of bed, limiting my choices and opportunities for the rest of my life; or I could choose to give it my absolute best shot and try to work out a way, no matter how long and how much effort it took.

To be honest, I was doubtful that I would ever be able to transfer, but I knew that if I didn't at least try I would look back on my life and wonder, *Was it ever possible?* I had to know if I could do it. To have pushed myself as far and as hard as I could, knowing in my heart that I couldn't have done any more, that I had tried my very best—only then could I accept and live with remaining dependent on others to cross this four-inch gap for the rest of my life.

The only way I could even consider this impossible goal was to break it down into smaller achievable goals, small goals that I could get my head around and have a go at.

At the Austin, Tracey showed me how to transfer: put my feet on the ground, move my body forward in the wheelchair seat, then move my bum across onto the bed, and finally lift my legs up. It sounds easy, but even if I managed to get onto the bed, I could never lift my legs—they were just too heavy, and I didn't have the strength.

The way I was shown didn't work for me. If I was to even have a slight chance, I had to do it differently. I had to work out a way that suited my physical capabilities.

During rehab at the Austin I had met Peter, another quad with years of experience in the business. He'd said that putting his legs up first was easier and gave him better balance. I decided to give it a go.

Now my new process was: lift my legs onto the bed, move my bum forward, and then slide across. That was it. Simple!

Every day I practised getting my legs on the bed. With the chair parallel to the bed, brakes on, I had to lift my left leg up first, then the right. They were so heavy. I struggled to just lift my left leg up halfway. Time and time again I tried. As soon as the leg was at forty-five degrees or so it felt like a rubber band was attached, springing it back no matter how hard I tried. For the next month I worked at it, over and over again, changing my technique to use the frame of the chair as a pivot point for my elbow to lever my leg up.

Then, unexpectedly, one day it seemed as if an invisible force grabbed my leg as I lifted, and with a quick flick it was up on the bed. Getting the right one up proved not to be as difficult due to the position and my right arm being stronger. Within days I had both legs up. My first big victory! I felt lightness in my body, a little sparkle of excitement mixed with a glimmer of hope that motivated me to keep going. I was a little closer to achieving my 'impossible' goal.

This was the easy part; but with that little bit of hope came a more positive outlook which whittled down the notion of impossibility, motivating me to attempt my next goal—getting my bum forward in the wheelchair. Putting my legs up first solved one problem but caused another: the rubber soles of my shoes prevented my feet from sliding on the sheets, making it much more difficult to slide my body forward. However, after a fair bit of yoga-like work twisting my legs to various angles that would make Elastic Woman flinch, I eventually managed to work out a way to remove my shoes.

To move my bum forward in the seat required me to throw the top half of my body forward, at the same time pushing off the right wheel and the bed for leverage with my arms. Gathering my strength, like a wildcat ready to explode onto its prey, I pushed with all my might. 'Faaark!' I yelped as the front of the chair spun away, my bum slid off the seat and I landed hard on the floor, my upper body falling backwards and my head hitting the bedside table. 'This is fuckin impossible,' I moaned and gave Frances, my carer, a roasting for not stopping the chair in time.

Putting the back of the wheels against the bedside table helped a little, but the front kept moving out. It was no use. I didn't have enough of my body working, or enough strength, to hold the chair and move forward, let alone slide across.

By getting my carer to hold the chair, I eventually managed to move my bum forward, requiring a lot of heaving, swearing and throwing myself forward like a pendulum. Although the cavernous four-inch gap between my chair and bed remained, with my carer holding my chair I surprised myself by being able to straddle it and drag myself to the other side. I felt stable enough that I wasn't going to fall, but more importantly, I began to think that maybe, just maybe, I might be able to do it. If I could just work out a way.

The hurdle that I couldn't overcome was stopping the front of the chair from moving away from the bed. I just didn't have the strength to hold it in place. I practised and practised over many months, trying different techniques, hoping that over time I might develop enough strength.

My motivation and sanity fluctuated like a roller coaster. My swearing and yelling didn't help my transfer, but it made me feel better. Each week I felt like giving up, especially when I couldn't see any progress; it was so disheartening. I was so close but no matter what I did, I just couldn't achieve my goal.

Frustrated and pissed off with trying and not getting anywhere, I'd leave it for a day or even a week if necessary, to recharge my mental energy, then have another go when I felt a little more positive. I was glad that I wasn't on my own. My family was supportive, letting me have a whinge and vent my frustration, then encouraging me to keep going. 'Do your best, that's all you can do,' Mum would say.

That is the one thing that has always been in the back of my mind: my parents' philosophy on learning, work and life in general: Do your best! Doing your best isn't just giving something a go. It's about harnessing your self-belief and exerting yourself physically, intellectually and mentally until you reach a point where you can hold your hand on your heart and say without any doubt that you have given one hundred percent.

I will do my best, I thought, *even if it kills me. I won't give up, I will stick at it until I've tried everything.*

Nearing the end of my stay at the Austin, a few other patients and I, assisted by volunteer nurses and orderlies, went on camp to Apollo Bay. I marvelled at Sandy's acrobatic strength and agility transferring a height of three feet from his wheelchair into a very high seat in a minibus. Secretly, I wanted to be as able as him, although I knew this wasn't going to happen. I hoped that miraculously I could do more than my level allowed, and transferring without the need for a device of some sort was all I wanted. But after all my attempts and frustrations over the many months, I eventually accepted that if I wanted to at least have a chance at achieving it, I needed to work out another way and do it differently.

I tried various ideas such as caster locks which hold the front casters of the wheelchair in place; they worked a little but not enough. My ideas got a little more elaborate, like devising an electric locking mechanism on the floor to hold the front of the chair.

I wouldn't say I was obsessed with trying to reach this goal, but working out a way to stop the chair from moving was consuming my waking thoughts. It was my last obstacle; I was so close.

As I sat next to my bed, looking at the floor in a daze from my last failed try and consequential disappointment, thoughts trickled through my mind as to how I could stop the front from moving. I suddenly experienced what could only be described as an epiphany.

The Holy Grail I had been looking for was so simple. A hook! *A simple hook!* I scolded myself. I couldn't believe I hadn't thought of it sooner—it was so obvious.

By bolting a hook to my bed, I could clip it onto the frame to hold my chair secure. It was brilliant! My heart raced with excitement; I was now so sure I could do it.

Dad found some scrap steel rod, bent it into shape, attached a strap made from an old seat belt and nailed it to the wooden bedframe.

I was impatient, ordering Dad to hurry up and move out of the way so I could try it.

Parking my chair next to the bed on a slight angle to minimise the gap between the chair and bed, I clipped the hook on easily. With my legs up, I threw myself forward—*whack, whack*—and pushed off the chair and bed, sliding my whole body forward. It held perfectly! Steadying myself, Dad ready to catch me if I fell, leaning forward I dragged my bum a little to test it. With the hook still holding, I pushed off with two short slides, dragging one bum cheek, then the other from the chair onto the bed.

'I DID IT!' I said, panting, with the biggest grin from ear to ear.

'Well done, David, that was really great,' Dad said, as happy as I was with the thought of no more late nights putting me to bed.

I needed my slide-board and some help to get back onto the wheelchair, which was a little difficult, but with some experimentation I managed to work it out and do it myself within a few weeks.

The four-minute mile was considered impossible to break until Roger Bannister broke it in 1954. Once that barrier was overcome, many started to surpass it, and now it's considered the benchmark for male middle-distance runners. The psychological barrier is far harder to break than the physical, but once it's broken the possibilities become endless.

When I achieved my impossible goal, conquering my Everest, the barriers that were stopping me from achieving more goals seemed to drop away more easily and quickly.

The hook idea was transferrable to the car. With a few modifications, I was soon getting myself in and out of the car. My challenge then was dismantling my wheelchair and getting it in and out as well. Initially it took me half an hour, but motivated by the possibilities and lots of practice, I got it down to under ten minutes.

I clearly remember the first time I realised my independence. I drove to my mate Dave's place for the evening and came home around midnight. Everyone was in bed, though Mum was probably lying awake waiting for me to yell out for help.

In the cold, I carefully got myself out of the car, making sure everything was in place so I didn't end up on the ground, pushed up the ramp, then onto the bed and undressed.

That night I didn't go to sleep straight away. I turned off the light and lay awake, relishing the satisfaction and contentment. It was the greatest sense of achievement I had ever experienced.

Phil was right. I didn't know myself after that. I wasn't the same person.

23

TRUE POTENTIAL

Thinking outside the square, doing it differently and never giving up until I had tried every possibility, was a turning point for me. Overcoming what I'd once perceived as an impossible obstacle changed my life.

Firstly, it gave me so much more independence, far more than I could have imagined. Not having to rely on my family to put me to bed was only one benefit, although a huge one. The priceless reward was freedom. The freedom to choose when I wanted to go to bed at night, or just to have a lie down in the middle of the day. It also gave me the choice to go out when and where I wanted in my car, independently.

I was free to go to the shopping centre, for a drive up the mountains, or down to the beach for a push along the foreshore. I could go out with friends as 'independent,' not needing someone to help me in and out of the car. Sure, there were always access issues where I needed a hand, but at least I could get there myself. I wasn't a burden. With my new freedom, I felt that I had regained a little more manliness, and I experienced a lift in my pride.

With my new freedom came the most important and greatest change in my life—a shift in my perspective. The experience changed the way I thought about challenges. It opened my mind to seeing the possibilities instead of only impossibilities.

When I say 'opened my mind' I mean, for example, saying 'maybe' rather than 'it's impossible.' It means being nonjudgemental, keeping all options open and viewing obstacles as opportunities for learning and growth.

An open mind is also about doing things differently, and not getting hung up on how other people do things. People are not robots; we are all different with varying skills and abilities. If performing a task one way doesn't work for you, try another way to achieve the outcome you want.

I couldn't transfer the way I was shown at the Austin with my legs down, so I changed my technique, putting my legs up on the bed first, which worked better for me. Developing the simple hook to lock my chair in place was a game-changer. Doing it differently enabled me to achieve the impossible.

But no matter how good your idea, or how much you want to achieve a goal, without taking action and, most importantly, persevering, the idea will remain just that—an idea.

The good news is that perseverance can be developed. By understanding your motivation for what you want to achieve, making a plan and setting clear measurable goals, expecting problems and trying different solutions, seeking out positive people who can give support; by focusing and making your action a habit, you will foster perseverance. It sounds complicated, but it is very easy when you start small and work up. Just remember to stick at it.

Elite athletes don't become the best just because of genetics, talent or luck; they do it by training and relentless perseverance. Working at it even when it becomes boring and repetitive, even when you have no idea whether the years of training will amount to anything, takes grit. Perseverance guarantees one thing—you become the best you can be.

It is said that Thomas Edison failed 999 times before he

succeeded in inventing a commercially viable light bulb on the 1000th attempt. When an experiment didn't work, he didn't view it as a failure, but as being one step closer to finding a solution.

Until you have investigated and tried all solutions, given it all you have, and you know in your heart that you have no more to give, you will never know whether your goal or dream was possible.

My change in perspective redefined what my true potential could be. The dreams or ambitions that may have seemed out of reach—whether starting a new career, living by myself or competing at the Paralympics—all now seemed possible.

THIRD LIFE

24

REBUILDING MY LIFE

I needed a goal, something to aim for, and I needed a plan. I needed to find a new map and a compass to know where I was heading in my life.

My goals had been to relearn basic, everyday living tasks; this had occupied my time and given me something to aim for each day, providing a reason to get out of bed. The more goals I achieved, the bigger the goals got, and so did my hopes for the future. I had progressed from relearning how to feed myself, to putting on a top, to driving, and now conquering my Everest—transferring into and out of my bed and car.

A faint glimmer of light shone in the distance. The hopelessness and emptiness I'd felt from not being able to see my future was fading. I started to think not just a day, a week or month ahead; I was now starting to consider years ahead, thinking of what seeds I needed to sow for my future. Although I didn't know what was around the corner, I felt hopeful and was excited by the possibilities ahead of me. For the first time, I knew I would have a plan.

Working, having a career, was important to me. Even as an eight-year-old I had an entrepreneurial streak. On weekends I would requisition Dad's lawn mower and Pete and I would push it around the streets, knocking on doors and offering our services.

With a couple of bucks in our pockets at the end of the day, tired and overheated, we would head to the local milk-bar. Sitting on the lawn mower in the afternoon sun, reminiscing on the day's events, we would stuff our mouths with lollies and biscuits, washing it all down with a bottle of Gold Medal blackcurrant soft drink. That was the life!

Working gave me purpose, a sense of self-worth, a means of becoming independent and being in control of my destiny. It was also a chance to regain something I had lost. I didn't know how I was going to work again, let alone what I'd do, but I wanted to earn enough money to one day move out of my childhood home and have my own life. This became my ultimate goal.

I couldn't go back to being a carpenter; I had to do something different. Given my physical limitations, I didn't know what was possible. The only thing I'd ever considered was carpentry.

I had never pictured myself sitting behind a desk, and I wasn't sure if it was something I could do, or even wanted to do.

I was hoping to do something that used my trade. Tom, my OT, arranged for me to have a chat with an estimator at AV Jennings, a large company that built houses. But I discovered that measuring and counting bits of materials off plans was not what I'd call exciting, and one other person in the game told me to avoid it: 'It's boring as bat shit!' I took his word for it.

On one of our port nights at Bwidgy's place, her husband Chambo, an engineer for an aviation company, introduced me to a very basic software program called CAD (Computer Aided Design). He showed me a few very simple things it could do, drawing lines at different angles using coordinates, a simple isometric box appearing on the screen. Off the shelf he pulled out a book with engineering designs. 'These were done with the CAD program,' he said. I was intrigued by its potential. *Maybe engineering was a possibility?* I thought, my mind ticking over. I'd never used a computer except for playing basic games like Asteroids at a mate's house, but I could always learn. I could see that engineering might provide many more opportunities to get a job with my disability. I had my plan, I'd give it a go.

I had never imagined going back to school and studying again; it was a little daunting considering my past school performances. I wouldn't say I hated school, but many aspects didn't interest me. I enjoyed sport, and even craft, but not the more academic side such as languages or maths. The traditional teaching method—rote learning, listening to the teacher talking about the subject, then doing exercises—was uninspiring and painfully boring to me, which made it a huge challenge to show even a slight interest. I wanted to be outside doing things that captivated me—like practical subjects. I loved using my hands to make or fix things.

My school results did not reflect my capabilities, but more so my lack of interest in and tolerance for a one-size-fits-all school system. The comments on my report cards usually went something like, 'David's results would be greatly improved if he spent less time talking in class.'

In Year 9, I transferred from Emmaus College to Syndal High School. It offered a few more practical subjects like woodwork and metalwork that caught my interest. By Year 10, I had decided I wanted to do a trade and be a carpenter.

I left Syndal High at the end of Year 10 and went to Holmesglen TAFE for Year 11, where the teaching methods were very different and we were treated more as adults, calling teachers by their first names. But most importantly, the teaching methods were practically based within subjects such as maths, English and science, with more emphasis on what would be of use with a trade career. We learned trade subjects such as graphic design, electronics, electrical work, carpentry, plumbing, fitting and machining and bricklaying, and I loved trying all these new practical activities.

I learnt far better using practical methods—getting out and being hands-on. I could see the usefulness of what we were learning. It was the first time I enjoyed and looked forward to going to school.

With my newfound level of motivation and interest, my report read: 'David has shown that he is very capable at almost anything he attempts.'

Before the end of the first semester I was one of the few students to get a carpentry apprenticeship with the Building Industrial Group Scheme.

Once I'd come to terms with having to go back to study, the idea of forging a new career was interesting and exciting. While I had changed a lot from my school days, the most important difference was that now I had a clear purpose and was fully motivated to rebuild my life.

Following the night with Chambo playing around with CAD, and after some research into courses, I decided to do design drafting. My dilemma was whether I should pursue architectural or engineering. My carpentry background would likely be an advantage with architectural; however, engineering offered more disciplines and possible opportunities for work.

Box Hill TAFE offered the architectural course I was interested in. Unsure how accessible the campus was, Mum came with me to lend me a hand.

'Hi, I'm David,' I said to the course coordinator as he approached us, putting out my hand to shake his.

'Hello David,' he said, as he pinched the ends of my fingers like he was picking up a dirty tissue.

'Mum just came to give me a hand to get around,' I said, clarifying that I was capable enough and didn't need my mum to come to the meeting. 'As I mentioned to you on the phone, I'm interested in doing the architectural drafting course, but I was wondering how the students did the drafting. My fingers don't work, so it'd be pretty hard for me to draw with a pencil and set squares,' I explained, raising my hands so he got the point.

'Yes, well, the students do all the drafting manually; it would be difficult for David,' he said to my mum.

'Could I do the drafting subjects on computer with Autocad?' I asked, asserting myself.

'Hmm, that would be difficult. I'm not sure how we could do that for David. We do have an introductory CAD subject, but we don't use it for the drafting subjects,' he said, again addressing my mum.

With the conversation going on above me, I felt like rolling into the corner and hiding in the shadows like a little kid. I felt invisible.

I'd gone into shops with 'uprights' before where the shop assistant spoke to them instead of me, which pissed me off; but this guy should have known better. I was shocked and very disappointed. This was my first real taste of ignorance—and it certainly wasn't to be the last.

I was hoping that my next meeting with Maurice, the coordinator of the engineering department at RMIT, would be less disappointing; however, I wasn't going to bet on it.

With Maurice dressed in a dated '80s multi-coloured pastel short-sleeve shirt and grey slacks, we sat in his office as I explained my situation. Listening intently and nodding, he said, 'We will do whatever you need so you can do the course.'

There was no decision to make: engineering it was.

The next two years spent earning my associate diploma of engineering went very quickly. True to Maurice's word, RMIT was very accommodating, enabling me to use Autocad for drafting. Within a faculty that showed consideration and respect, I excelled. My grades reflected my abilities and motivation, winning me an award for best academic performance.

25

WORLD CHAMPIONSHIPS

At the start of my studies in 1992 I was back playing wheelchair rugby every Wednesday night. As a 0.5, I was a blocker, stopping the opposition's ball handler from scoring a goal. The high-pointers got the glory while the low-pointers were the quiet achievers.

It had become an important part of my life; it was like playing football again. Wheelchair rugby was exciting and I enjoyed working as one of a team, while the crowd's support and cheering pumped my adrenalin. And I really enjoyed the contact, especially giving a good hit and stopping the more able players; it was very satisfying. It could be fast-moving, with the players 'sprinting' up the court, as well as requiring strategic tactics using different plays to score, as in basketball.

Apart from the enjoyment, sport got me fitter, which then made my life easier—whether it was pushing my wheelchair or doing everyday things like putting on a jumper. Sport also introduced me to other people with varying levels of quadriplegia, opening my eyes to how they did daily tasks, which gave me ideas to try to increase my independence.

I'd left the Austin Hospital with a writing splint that looked like part of an unfinished prosthetic hand. It was very bulky and cumbersome to use, and not that easy to whip it out of my pocket for an autograph without getting a few stares, so I rarely wrote. At the end of a Wednesday evening rugby night, I became intrigued with the way Mick (Super Quad) was writing on a piece of paper. He didn't have a Frankenstein-looking splint, so I asked, 'How are you holding the pen, Mick?'

'I stick it between my fingers. Good to get a pen you don't need to press down hard, though,' he said, holding up his fist with the pen jammed between his pointer and middle finger.

When I got home, I found a pen with a thick body to give me better grip, stuck it between my fingers, and it worked a treat. It was much easier to write with, and I didn't need to take the bulky strap-on appendage around with me anymore. It was small things like this that helped me to achieve more in the early days.

My family was always positive and supportive, but getting beyond the four walls at home and being around motivated people in similar situations made a big difference to me. It helped nurture a positive outlook, increased my confidence and generated internal energy. Being with positive and motivated people inspired me to push myself further. I was one of the least physically able most of the time, trying to compete with the more able players. I had to continually push myself harder, always one hundred percent effort of my six percent capacity, just to keep up and be competitive. This grind of continually pushing myself was tough, but through sport and consistently working towards my daily goals, the practice of pushing myself started to become ingrained—it became a habit, which has served me to this day.

In 1994 I made the Victorian team for the National Wheelchair Games. It was my first Nationals and I was so excited to be playing teams from other states, a big step up from the local competition. The team to beat was New South Wales. They played a very tight, strategic game; we gave them a good run for their money, but they beat us. We finished with silver, still a very respectable result.

These Nationals gave me a 'taste for blood,' so to speak. When we played South Australia, I had a lot of court time. It was a battle between two evenly matched teams, and it came down to the last few seconds when SA scored a goal, drawing the game. With another minute of overtime put on the clock to sort out a winner, we went back into battle. It was incredibly intense, both sides urgent to score. The game was frantic, the ball bouncing from player to player, the sound of crunching metal as chairs bounced off each other, as we all desperately tried to get the ball over the goal line.

We were up by one point, thinking it was in the bag, when, in the dying seconds, a fast player from South Australia broke loose and caught the ball just before crossing the goal line, drawing the score again. With another minute on the clock, we drew again.

With sweat pouring off those who could sweat, both teams were running on adrenalin. As we went into the third time-on, the noise from the crowd was deafening: it was like being at an MCG grand final. I managed to lock away SA's 1-point player, who was quicker than me, from the goals so as to mismatch the opposition. I struggled to hold him using my last reserves of strength, the sides of our chairs locked together, as the seconds ticked down for another draw. The crowd was in a screaming frenzy. 'Down court, down court!' I yelled, but I couldn't even hear my voice above the deafening roar of the crowd. In the dying seconds Peter, our fast 2-pointer, broke away, his arms pumping like pistons as he raced down court. Baden smashed the ball, bouncing ahead of him towards our goals. 'Go, go, go!' we screamed, our hearts in our mouths. As the last second on the clock flashed to zero, Peter threw himself forward onto his knees, then picked up the rolling ball with his fingertips just as he rolled across the goal line, the siren and umpire's whistle screeching in unison. Laurie, the umpire, hesitated for a split second before his hand went up. The roar and screams from the crowd were thunderous. We had won!

On court we wanted to annihilate the opposition, but sitting in the hotel lobby afterwards having a few drinks and reminiscing about our day's game, some of the more experienced players gave advice to the newbies. 'You did some great picks, Dave. If you sit behind the outside player in the goal 'D,' you can come in behind to get a gap for a score,' said Locky, one of the better NSW players against whom we got silver. With the game being so new, we were all eager to learn and share knowledge to improve everyone's performance. This would lead to better competition, and we'd have loads more fun. Many of us became good friends, looking forward to the next competition. Some of these would become my teammates at the 1995 World Wheelchair Rugby Championships in Switzerland following successful tryouts in Sydney.

Two days before I was to leave for Switzerland, Nancy, one of my carers who did four days a week, told me, 'I'm going to resign when you get back.'

'Oh ... why?'

'I've decided I don't want to do this anymore,' she said.

'Why's that?'

'I need a change.'

'OK, if that's what you want,' I said, and left it at that.

The following morning, she didn't turn up. I was freaking out because I was leaving the next day and had so much to do. I called her a number of times but no answer. Mum helped me get up that morning and pack but luckily Joyce, one of my past carers, was available and willing to help me out the next morning to get me on the plane.

Sitting in the middle row of the plane between two of the biggest guys on the team—George, our most able player, and Steve—I was squashed in like a passenger on a Tokyo train in rush hour, unable to move for over twelve miserable hours from Hong Kong to Switzerland. They both slept most of the way; I didn't sleep a wink.

Our team had five support staff, Phil, our coach, also in a wheelchair, and nine players including me, the only Victorian player. Travelling with the team was easy; the staff gave us a hand when we needed it and did all my care. Most of the players could look after themselves: it was only me and Wayne from NSW, the other 0.5-point player, who relied on significant help.

The tournament was held in Nottwil at the Swiss Paraplegic Centre, an amazing futuristic facility, even back in 1995. The hospital there was a world-class leader in spinal rehabilitation set in the picturesque green, grassy countryside on the shores of Lake Sempach. The facility had everything, including a basketball court that we were to play on, and even an athletics track. The court was a low-impact surface that made it like pushing on a soft mat with little roll-through. I was going to struggle. My rugby chair was my old everyday wheelchair, lowered and with modified footplates, bent back towards the frame to make it a little shorter and provide more of a bull bar for picking and blocking the opposition. Our equipment looked amateurish compared to some of the other teams, such as the USA. They had purpose-built rugby wheelchairs, specifically designed for the players' roles—far superior to what we were using.

Our accommodation during the tournament was underground in the bunker run by the Swiss army next to the spinal facility. 'Einezwanzig,' I'd say to the soldier at the checkpoint as he ticked me off on the register to let me enter the side of the hill. When the lights were turned off, it was pitch black; I wasn't even sure if my eyes were open or closed.

Eight teams participated; from memory it was Australia, New Zealand, Sweden, Switzerland, USA, Canada, Norway and England. We played a round robin, facing each team once before the knockout finals.

It was hard going on the soft court, with the surface so slow that when I pushed on the wheels, I'd only roll a metre: it was as if my tyres were flat and I had trouble keeping up. The play would go one way, I'd lean forward pumping my chicken arms as fast as I could, but as soon as I caught up, it would move to another position, like a shoal of fish avoiding its predator. I realised I had to change my game. By sitting back from the play a little, seeing who was free or had a clear line, I could anticipate where the play would go, then sneak in and attack a higher-point player to block or slow him down.

Playing against the USA and Canada, the best teams in the world at the time, opened my eyes to how good we could be. It was as if they could read our minds; we'd box them in but as soon as we thought we had them cornered, a player would launch the ball to another faster player who was motoring around the court like a cruising shark, and would chase the ball down and score. At times, with their fantastic ball skills it seemed like they were playing keepings-off, passing the ball around the court to moving players. The USA 0.5-point player was more like a 1-pointer: he was fast, strong, and could read the play like a clairvoyant, something to which I aspired.

We battled in each game; we had some wins but more losses than we'd hoped. Although we finished fifth, our goal was to finish in the top six, securing our place for the Paralympics in 1996. Playing against the best teams in the world was tough, but it was a fantastic experience. I learnt a great deal from the tactics and strategies used by opposition players, in particular 0.5-point players. It was a great lesson in what was necessary to be the best.

Wheelchair rugby was going to be a demonstration sport in the 1996 Atlanta Paralympics, and I wanted a spot on the team.

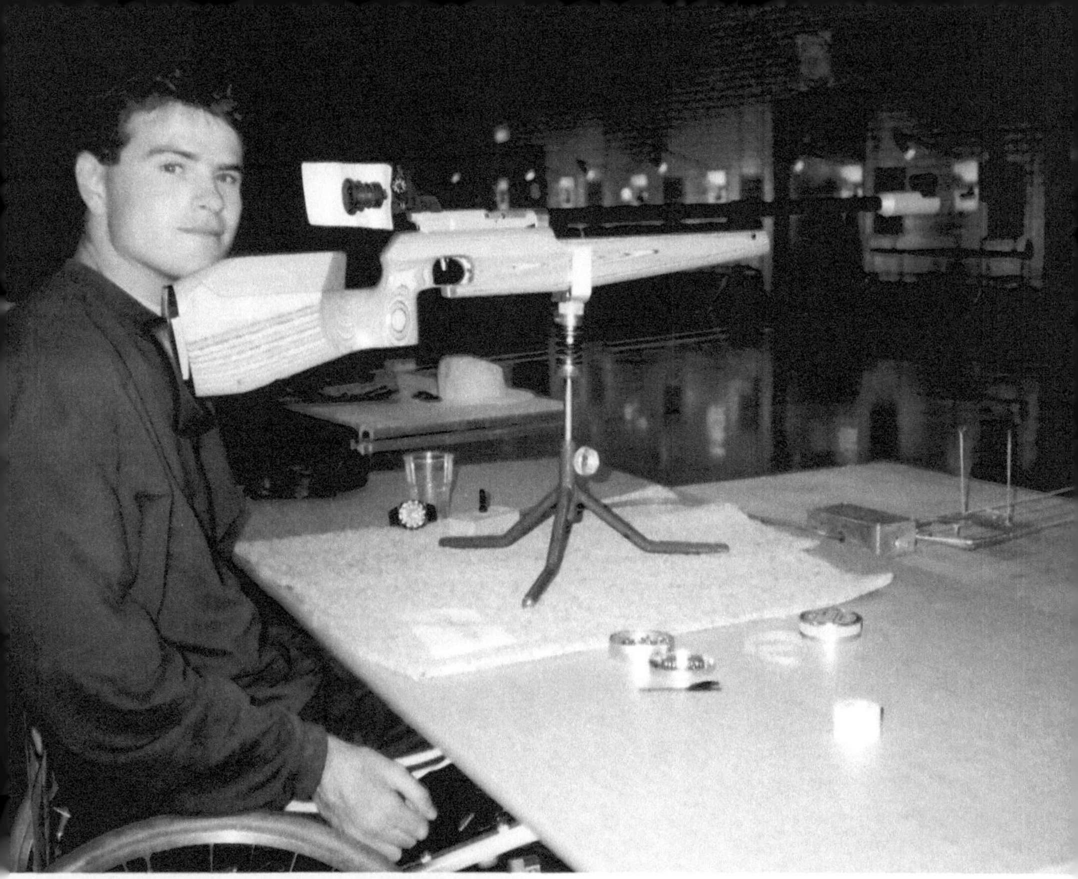

Competing at the 1991 Oceania Shooting Championships in Adelaide, South Australia. I used a shooting stand with a spring to help hold the weight of the gas-powered rifle.

Surprising myself, I won a gold medal in the 3 x 40 (Standing, Kneeling and Prone x 40 shot for each position), at the 1991 Oceania Shooting Championships in Adelaide, South Australia.

The hook attached to my bed which holds the wheelchair in position, stopping it from moving, enables me to transfer. It was such a simple idea, and one that changed my life. I use a similar one on my car to transfer in and out.

The Jacka family in the early 90s. Madeleine, Kathryn, Elizabeth (EJ), Marguerite, Brian (Dad), Me and Roberta (Mum)

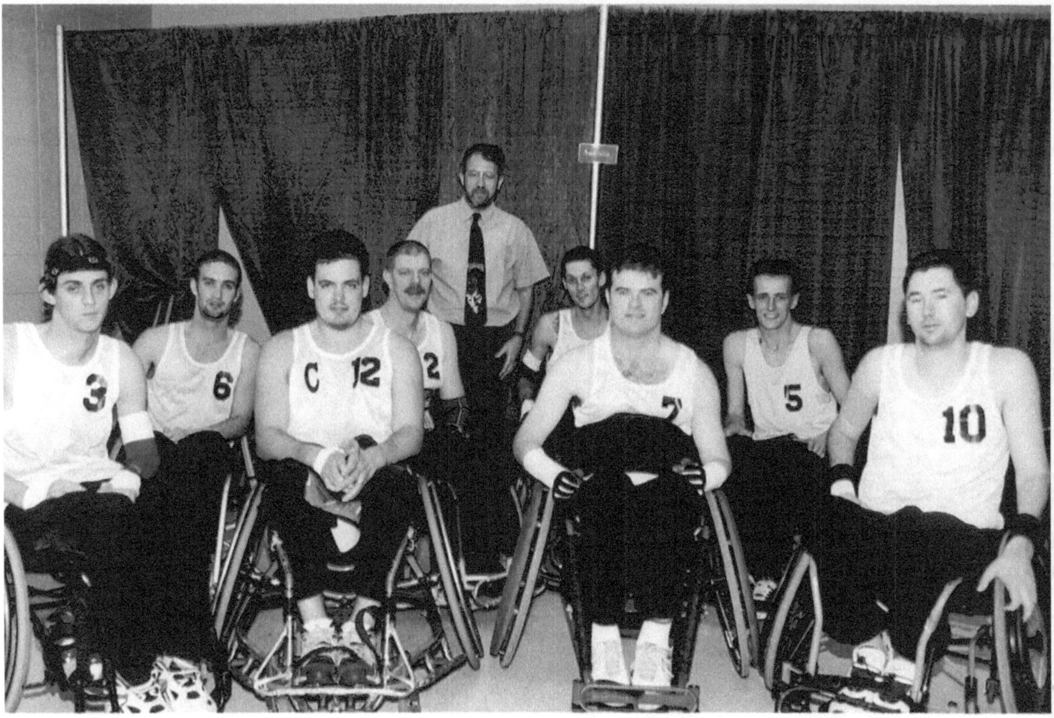

Australian Wheelchair Rugby team at the 1996 Atlanta Paralympics.
R-L: Andrew, Rod, Steve, Baden, Darryl (coach), Peter (Locky), Me, Brett, and Garry. George had gone back to Australia following his injury.
Photo: John Sherwell/Sport The Library

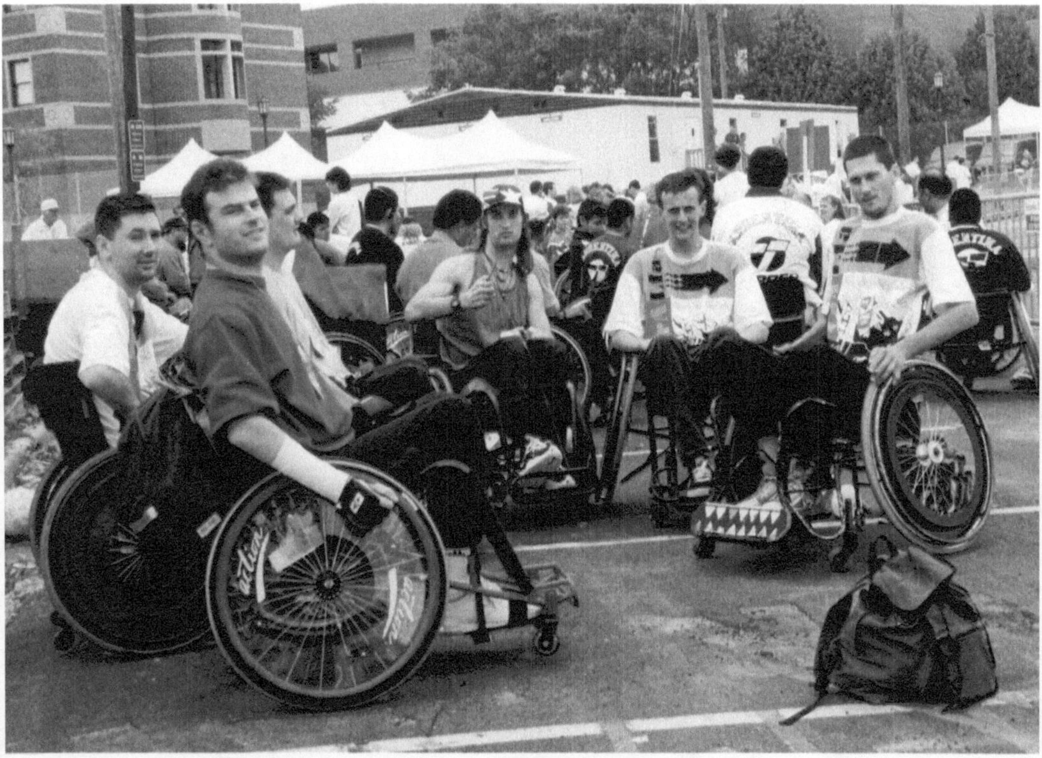

The team strapped up and in our rugby chairs. It was a long wait for the bus to arrive to take us to the training venue. 1996 Atlanta Paralympics.

When the Victorian Paralympic athletes returned from Atlanta, the premier Jeff Kennett presented the team with the key to the city (Melbourne) at a celebratory event.

Ripping up the half-pipe at Mt Hotham in 2004 with Nick.
Photo: Able Management Group

Me in the Bi-Unique sit ski with Nick assisting as my ski guide, Mt Hotham in 2004.
Photo: Able Management Group

The smile on my face said it all! I had just completed my first successful Trial Instructional Flight (TIF) with Steve Ruffels (right) using my base-bar adaptation.

Left: The start of training in my modified Airborne Edge X 582 microlight trike. The cockpit had my new improved base-bar adaptation with push buttons for the throttle control. My left hand is on the ground steering lever, and the go-cart seat with harness provided good lateral support. The magneto (kill) switches are on the right side out of view.

Right Top: Steve Ruffels and I celebrating with champagne. My boyhood dream of flying had become a reality, as I completed my first solo flight on 14th February 2006. It was a wonderful achievement for Steve, with full credit for his open-mindedness which gave me the opportunity to gain the gift of flight. *Photo: Lisa Ruffels*

Right Below: As the evening light faded, the personal significance of my achievement was still sinking in. *Photo: Lisa Ruffels*

Final approach at Porepunkah Airfield, Victoria, February 2006.
Photo: The Border Mail

Pulling off a smooth landing on the grassed runway at Porepunkah Airfield, Victoria, February 2006. *Photo: The Border Mail*

26

A JOB

With my course and the World Championships behind me, I now wanted a job to start the next phase of rebuilding my life—the tracksuit pant quad uniform replaced with a suit and tie.

Over the past year, I had done some small contract work at home for the aviation company Chambo worked for, drawing up test equipment on Autocad. Just the idea of finding a job was scary, as I was rolling into the unknown. I didn't know what it would be like, what obstacles and challenges I would have to deal with: it was daunting. Where did I even start?

There were very few advertised jobs for a design draftsman, so I decided my best chance was to send my CV to engineering companies. I didn't know what else to do. The dilemma of what I should say in my cover letter, whether I was in a wheelchair or with quadriplegia, was a drawn-out debate with my parents. They believed I should be upfront. I didn't want to give a false impression, and if I rolled up for an interview my situation would become obvious, so upfront it was.

As the weeks passed, I received a couple of responses that said, 'Thank you for your CV; however, we have no positions, we will keep it on file.' The rest of my queries were obviously ignored.

An aeronautical engineering company advertised for a junior

person in the role of technical officer. With my long-time interest in planes and flying, and having the necessary qualifications for the role, it was a perfect fit for me. I spoke to the interviewer on the phone and he seemed impressed enough to invite me in for a formal interview.

In the interviewer's office we spent half an hour chatting, which seemed to be going really well; I even thought I'd possibly landed the job. At the end of the interview he said, 'Would you like to have a look around the office?'

'Sure, that would be great,' I said, now confident I had it in the bag.

I'd been given a plastic security tag when I arrived and had it sitting on the table in front of me. As we were leaving, I reached to pick it up. The table had a brown woodgrain Laminex top, which was very slippery. As I tried to pick up the tag, it kept sliding away and I just couldn't get a good hold, fumbling with my gummy fingers. I noticed the guy looking intently at my hands as I struggled; he seemed fixated. *Fuck it*, I thought, and out of frustration I slid it over and used both hands to pick it up.

He showed me round a little, but I sensed the mood had changed. Instead of the free-flowing conversation, he started asking a lot of questions that felt more like an interrogation.

'How would you type on a computer?' he asked.

'I have a pen with a rubber nib that I hold between my fingers on my left hand and I use the pointer finger on my right. I can type really well. I also use a trackball instead of a mouse. It's not a problem,' I said.

'How do you write?'

I demonstrated with a pen, holding it between two fingers as Mike had shown me.

'How would you put together a report?' he queried.

I did my best to explain how I could do most tasks but might need a little help occasionally with things that required good working fingers, but I knew I wouldn't get the job. No matter what I said, nothing would change the way he now perceived me. Did he not think I could do the job, or was he afraid to employ me because if it didn't work out, it would be difficult to get rid of me? I really didn't know. Either way, what really pissed me off was that I knew I could do it; I just needed to be given a chance to prove myself.

I felt so deflated, as this was the best and only chance I'd had so far. I had never experienced such closed-mindedness. I was angry and felt demoralised. I wanted to quit.

My parents continued to encourage me, urging me to keep going as something was bound to happen eventually. It was all about perseverance.

I continued to call up and send off CVs to various engineering consultancy firms, but with no luck for the next six months.

I removed the word 'quadriplegia' from my cover letter. My thinking was that when people hear or read the word 'quadriplegia,' they immediately imagine a head sitting on top of an immobile body, unable to do anything. But if I simply said 'wheelchair,' they would probably think I was a more physically able person with paraplegia.

As the months passed, the frustration and hopelessness accumulated to all-consuming doubt. But when I was almost at rock bottom, a lifeline was thrown to me. Malcolm, the manager of the building service department at the engineering consultancy firm Connell Wagner, called me up one afternoon and invited me in for a chat.

Out of desperation, I had sent a few CVs to firms asking for work experience only. I figured that if no one was interested in giving me a job, I'd at least be better off having some work experience. I had inadvertently sent my CV to the managing director and when he saw it, he told Malcolm to get me in.

I could tell that Malcolm and Russell, the lead draftsman,

were a little hesitant but after explaining that I only wanted work experience, and with the incentive of employer assistance available from the CES, they gave me a chance. I was to start in January 1996 for one month only.

Russell was patient and a really nice guy, as were most of the people I worked with there. He took me under his wing and taught me the fundamentals of drafting and how they did things in building services, where they designed air-conditioning systems. It was very different from what I had learnt in my course, and because the time spent on a drawing cost money, you had to be very fast and do only what was needed.

I worked hard, trying my best to pick up the knowledge and increase my skills, hoping they could see my potential.

When I was given a small drafting job, I made sure I got it done on time, even if I had to stay back late to finish. Although there were no jobs available with the lull in work at the time, I hoped that if I could prove my worth, they might take me on if a vacancy came up.

The month became two, and at the end of the third in April, Malcom called me into his office. 'David, how do you feel about working here full-time?'

I finally had a job. It was on a basic junior drafter's wage, only a little more than the pension, but it was a job. They had given me a chance and I had proven my worth. It was all I needed.

27

PARALYMPICS

Tryouts for the 1996 Paralympic wheelchair rugby team were in Sydney in early 1996. Dozens of players from the various states turned up to have a shot. The weekend was hot, the sun streaming through the open doors blinding me as it reflected off the shiny wooden floors of the stadium.

The tryouts consisted of two exhausting days pushing up and down the court doing drills, sprints and simulated games. I was up against some tough competition for the 0.5 position, so I had to make sure I gave it all that I had, continuously pushing myself flat out, unsure how long I could keep it up with my arms burning and nauseated from the pain. All I knew was that I couldn't stop. I couldn't be seen as a weaker player.

On the second day, I had a magical session with Rod, a 2.5-point Victorian player (reasonable balance, fully functioning arms and semi-working fingers). We were doing offensive plays in a practice game; I was working with Rod to try and get him in to score as, being a more able player, he was the ball handler. Every time we went in, he drew the play, then I went in, smash! With the opposition player blocked, Rod would swing around through the gap behind me—a trick I had learnt from Locky at the Nationals—and scored. It just clicked; it was if we could read each other's minds, and we could not be beaten. The defensive team looked incompetent—it was awesome!

Following the months of hope and anticipation, the day arrived in April when the team was announced. We sat around the TV screen in a hotel organised by the Australian Paralympic Committee in Melbourne, waiting to see if our names scrolled up on the screen. My name came up in the list. I had made it! I'd never dreamt I would compete at the highest level of sporting competition and play against some of the legends of the game.

Of eight players on the Australian team, I was the only 0.5. Baden, a 2-pointer, also the oldest member of the team in his forties, brought a little more stability with his maturity; the rest of us were in our mid- to late-twenties. Rod, who used to be a competition motocross rider until his luck ran out, was a 2.5-pointer, the third Victorian. Steve 2.5, and George 3.0, both from South Australia, were in; they were like conjoined twins, always sharing a room. Garry, a 1-pointer from the ACT, was soft spoken, a little more serious than most of the guys. The boys from New South Wales—Peter (Locky) 2.5, Andrew 1.5 and on reserve Brett 2.0—were all really skinny; they could have passed for brothers. Andy was really nice, gentle and quiet; Locky with tats looked a tad rough but was a great bloke; and Brett was quieter, a tactician on the game. Our coach was Darryl, also from South Australia, with an old-school 'get in and give 'em hell' approach. It was a great bunch of blokes and very supportive of each other. We came from different backgrounds, and it's unlikely our paths would have crossed in our previous lives. Our passion for the game was the common link that brought us together. Looking at the team, you wouldn't have thought we were elite athletes, a few blokes puffing on cancer sticks in a rest break, but when it came down to business, we were very serious, giving it everything we had. We were determined—we wanted to win.

Following selection, it was full on. With my new job at Connell

Wagner, it was a struggle working full-time and putting in the necessary training. I worked five days a week, I went to the gym three evenings a week and on the remaining nights, rugged up against the cold, I pushed up and down the hills in the dark streets of Glen Waverley, keeping an eye on the cars so I didn't get hit. On weekends, Baden and I practised our wheelchair rugby skills. I spent all my time either working or training. I shut out all other distractions because I had to be totally focused. I wanted to give it my best shot.

Each month we travelled to Adelaide for a training camp, flying there on the Friday and returning exhausted on the Sunday night. Darryl had a budget for only accommodation and flights, so without team support personnel I had to hire a carer in Adelaide to put me to bed and get me up in the morning. By going through an agency, I never knew who I'd get. This made getting up in the morning a very slow process, as I had to instruct the carer on the routines. And on a couple of occasions, the carer didn't show.

'It's David here, are you coming this morning? You were meant to be here an hour ago!' I'd say on the phone. I was usually greeted with a groggy and hungover, 'Aw, shit, sorry, I'll be there soon.' I'd then have to get myself to the venue in a taxi, and Darryl wasn't too happy when I rolled up late.

At least the airline staff gave me much more help than they do today—lifting me from my wheelchair into the aisle chair, then from the aisle chair into the aircraft seat. Now, with stricter OH&S policies, they aren't allowed to provide lifting assistance, which requires me to travel with someone.

When I fly, I stay in my wheelchair until I am at the door of the plane before being lifted into the aircraft aisle chair. The aisle chair is a very narrow wheelchair that fits between the seats of the plane. At the destination, the crew call the ground staff to get my wheelchair from the hold so I can get into it at the door of the plane instead of sitting in the very uncomfortable aisle chair for the next hour while they search for it at baggage. It generally goes to plan, but not always.

Coming back from Adelaide one Sunday evening on a quiet flight, I got talking to a friendly and attractive flight attendant. I made a few witty jokes which made her laugh—a good sign, I thought, Rod and Baden offering their encouragement. When we landed, I asked her to make sure my wheelchair was at the door of the plane and to put my special air cushion on the seat.

She went ahead as I was wheeled down the aisle, my shoulders bouncing off each seat like a pinball.

'How does your cushion go on your chair?' she asked.

'It just sits on top,' I said, thinking that my potential new girlfriend wasn't very bright. As soon as I saw the wheelchair, I went red with embarrassment while a few of the flight attendants stood around scratching their heads.

'That's not my wheelchair!' I blurted, staring at the commode wheelchair: a toilet seat on wheels. I never got her number.

At least access on and off planes had been stepped up at most airports by 1996, making travel a little less challenging for wheelchair users. My first experience travelling to Perth and then Port Hedland in 1990 to see my sister Marg was an unexpected accessibility adventure. In Perth, I was loaded into a food van to get me on and off the plane, and in Port Hedland they drove a forklift up to the aircraft door and wheeled me onto a pallet. The pallet itself wasn't so bad, but looking down without siderails one storey up made me a little uncomfortable as the forklift jerked and rocked as it backed away from the plane. But the worst was in Bali, with four small Balinese ferrying me in the aisle wheelchair down the very, very steep steps of the mobile stairs onto the tarmac. The two guys at the front kept lowering the front too far. 'Lift up, lift up!' I yelled as I struggled to keep my grip on the backrest. If I'd lost hold, I would have surely ended up somersaulting down the stairs and sprawling onto the hot tarmac like a steak slapped onto a BBQ hotplate.

The day in early August 1996 when we boarded the plane wearing our blue, white and red uniforms was the day the Paralympics became reality. We flew to Birmingham, Alabama, first for a week-long training camp at the Lakeshore Foundation—a rehabilitation organisation that supported people with physical disabilities—then we were bused to Atlanta, Georgia, for the Paralympic Games.

On our first day of training in Birmingham, we started with some warm-up drills, the standard three-man weaves. Steve was in the centre passing the ball to George on the outside, who threw it to Rod on the other side. As he came in behind Steve, George's front footplate clipped the back of Steve's wheel. His chair tipped forward, landing upside down, and his knee crashed onto the hardwood floor, making a dull thud.

'Good one, Georgie, bit unco, mate,' a few of us said, laughing, giving him shit for a rookie mistake. We got back into training and didn't think anything of it.

At the team meeting the following morning, Darryl delivered the devastating news: 'Guys, George's knee swelled up like a football last night, we took him to the hospital and they said he has broken his kneecap.'

'Fuck, you're kidding!' we chorused.

'Unfortunately, this means he won't be able to play and will need to go home,' said Darryl.

The room fell silent.

'How's he doing?' asked Baden, always concerned with other people's welfare.

'Yeah, he's fine, pretty sore though, but as you'd expect, he's very disappointed.'

My heart sank. I felt terrible for George and could only imagine how devastated he was. As the reality and repercussions of the situation sunk in, a sickening feeling welled up inside me. I knew that we were screwed—not that anyone would admit it. George was the most able player on our team; he had the most function, more like a paraplegic with good trunk function and semi-gummy hands, than a quad. He was our grunt, the brute force and speed we needed to be competitive. This was the worst thing that could happen so close to the Games.

'Who will we get to replace him?' someone asked.

'I've spoken to Brett; he'll fly out tomorrow and get here the day after that,' said Darryl.

Brett was a great strategist but, being a 2-pointer, he could never fill George's wheels.

We continued at the training camp; the local wheelchair rugby team helped us out and played a few games against us for practice, some of which we barely won. As we sat outside on the grass in the warm sun after almost being beaten by the local team, Locky said, 'What the fuck are we doing? We were almost beaten by those guys.' We knew we should be doing better. I guess losing a teammate we had come to know, trust and rely on threw us into a downward spiral, draining our confidence and competitive spirit.

Losing George also meant that the combinations of players originally planned wouldn't work now: a new strategy was required. This change impacted me significantly: I wouldn't be getting as much game time as I'd hoped.

After the training camp we went to Atlanta, staying at Georgia Tech accommodation units with the other teams. Our unit had three bedrooms big enough to hold our whole team. Darryl and our support staff—big Andre, whom I knew as an orderly when I was at the Austin Hospital, and Rod—stayed in another room.

In the USA, none of our accommodations had wheel-in showers;

the showers were over the bath. Each morning, with sweat pouring off Andre's balding head, the few scraggy hairs tickling my nose, I'd wrap my arms around his neck, and with a grunt he'd stand all six-foot-three of me up and lower me into the bath; then, when I was finished, out again. Not an easy thing to do.

Garry had been to a number of the previous Paralympics playing table tennis, and he painted a picture of how awesome the Games would be. But our first night didn't match his story. When we arrived, a few things weren't yet in place, such as our blankets, so we used towels to keep warm. I remember hearing that the Paralympics were almost cancelled as they didn't have the necessary funding, but thankfully, they were eventually bailed out.

The Olympics was largely funded through corporate sponsorship, a major sponsor being Coca-Cola. At least everyone at the Paralympics got an endless supply of Coke and Powerade from the drink machines.

Each country stayed in a different part of the complex. It was fascinating to see what equipment was being used in the other countries. There were wheelchair designs I'd never seen before and other bits of equipment that gave us good ideas to bring home. Some teams we knew very well, such as the New Zealanders, who were our rivals from past tournaments and a very good team.

We caught up with a few players when we arrived, chatting about their preparations and a team-bonding session.

'We thought we'd get a tattoo,' said one player, pulling up his sleeve to show the five Olympic rings inked into his skinny forearm.

We looked at each other and smiled.

He went on to say, 'After we had it done, we realised it was the wrong symbol. It should have been the three teardrops, you know, for the Paralympics.'

'Aw bugga!' said Baden.

'Yeah, I know,' he said, his face long with disappointment.

In the heat and humidity of the evening, with thousands of people cheering the players of the various countries, I wheeled into the huge stadium for the opening ceremony—a thrilling and uplifting experience. Christopher Reeve was the MC for the night. He had recently put a lot of time and effort into getting spinal-cord injury into the spotlight as well as money into research for a cure, which was fantastic. The more coverage and awareness, the better. But one thing he said perplexed me, and stuck in my mind. During his address he said words to the effect of: 'You've come here to win gold … I want to walk again.'

Unless I had heard incorrectly, given the company he was addressing, it seemed a little out of step, so to speak. The people in the stadium weren't held back by their circumstances; instead, we were celebrating life, our goals being to be our country's best in our chosen sport and make the most of our lives.

I've met a couple of people over the years who couldn't move on, desperate to reclaim what they had lost, trying so hard with positive thinking, special exercises or anything else they'd heard could work. But eventually their worlds caved in when, after years of hoping and waiting, the hoped-for cure or miracle didn't eventuate. By then it was too hard and too late to attempt some of the things they could possibly have achieved early on, despite their disabilities.

This reminds me of a guy I once knew with paraplegia, who wanted to walk so badly that he had handrails installed in his home. He'd strap on callipers to lock his legs straight, stand himself up and drag his stiff, rigid legs around by the use of his arms on the rails. He spent years dragging his lifeless legs along the ground, willing them to move. In the end this destroyed his shoulders and he ended up far worse off in a power chair, unable to transfer himself and needing carers. It was only a few years before his death that he finally came to terms with his situation.

A few years ago, I had a carer say to me, 'You're not walking because you gave up!'

What the fuck! I thought. After a stunned moment, taking a few deep breaths, I calmly asked how she came to such a conclusion. 'Well, if you believed you would walk then you would,' she said. Maybe having a crushed spinal cord has something to do with it! The reality is that once your spinal cord is severely damaged, there is little chance of recovery, and no amount of believing will change the outcome.

I've certainly had my moments, when I wished my accident never happened and I could be what I once was. But living in hope to the extent that it becomes an affliction, an all-consuming obsession, putting life on hold in the hope of getting better, whether through a miracle or cure is, I feel, such a waste of a person's potential and life. Walking is overrated anyway!

Wishing for how things were in the past, or dreaming, hoping for a better future that is completely out of a person's control, stops us from getting on with living. Don't get me wrong, it's necessary to reflect on the past; that's how we learn and grow. And we need to think about the future to plan our lives and nurture dreams of what we want to achieve. But what's really important is to focus our energies and thoughts on what we *can* control to enable us to live a full and enjoyable life.

Early on after my accident, I chose to put my energy into having the best life I could instead of into things I couldn't control. I wanted to live each moment as fully as possible, not just to survive, but to thrive. If a cure were to come along one day, great. But until then I would focus on having as many experiences as possible and living a rich and fulfilling life.

No matter our situation, each of us has a choice over our actions and what we get out of life. As Andy Dufresne says in *The Shawshank Redemption*: 'I guess it comes down to a simple choice really: get busy living or get busy dying.'

The first day of training in Atlanta was abysmal due to transport delays, but they soon got organised and it was much better after that. The bus ride to the stadium wasn't the usual tourist route; it passed through some of the poorer parts of Atlanta that made me appreciate where I lived back home.

My parents had come over for the Games, and it was really nice to have their support. I wanted them to see me play. We were playing against five teams: New Zealand, Great Britain, Canada, USA and Sweden. It was a round robin, two games per day with one on the third day. We'd play each team once then the top four qualified for the finals. Without George we were seriously down on manpower. To beat the USA or Canada was a tough ask, but we hoped we had a chance against Great Britain, New Zealand and Sweden.

New Zealand, Canada and the USA beat us solidly. We were up on Great Britain. The game was intense, my nerves on edge from the sidelines. One missed opportunity caused us to lose the ball with Great Britain scoring. A missed catch caused another turnover to Great Britain, which was the beginning of the end for us, the frustration building with each simple mistake. It was like watching a car crash that you want to look away from but can't. When the final siren went, any hope we had instantaneously turned to disappointment: we'd lost by one point. This was the most disheartening day of the Games. It's not so bad being beaten well by a good team, but to lose when we were so close was painful. With all the training and time taken out of my life, this sort of ending was heartbreaking.

Our final game against Sweden would decide who would finish last. We were like an arthritic old dog taken out to the paddock and put out of our misery. We lost by four points.

The disappointment of not winning was one thing, but the salt in my wound was that my parents, who had travelled so far, hardly saw me play because I didn't get much court time.

As a team, we did what we could with the cards we were dealt. I know in my heart we all gave it one hundred percent, and that was all we could do. To have won a medal would have been the icing on the cake. I am very proud to have gone into battle with this eclectic group of men who'd dedicated themselves to representing their country and who gave it their best shot. It just wasn't our time.

FOURTH LIFE

28

MY HOME

Six years earlier I began to put in motion the steps I hoped would lead to my ultimate goal of independence: moving out of my childhood home. Now, with a secure job, I could seriously consider buying a home that I could modify to suit my needs and live as independently as possible.

Although I had all the support and freedom in the world at my parents' place, I couldn't feel that I had fully grown up as long as I was under their roof. I needed to cut the psychological umbilical cord to feel fully in charge of my life and destiny.

Fortunately, Mum loved looking at houses, which meant I could outsource the bulk of the research. It took over two years of looking at dozens of houses, with many weekends ending in deflation as the houses were either not suitable to modify for wheelchair access or were out of my price range. But persistence paid off and I finally found what I was looking for. With some help from my parents, a cream-and-green old Edwardian house with a cottage garden in the inner suburbs of Melbourne was mine—and the bank's. After another year to complete the modifications—converting a bedroom into a bathroom and roll-in wardrobe, changing the kitchen and door handles and installing ramped paths—the day arrived when my ultimate goal became a reality. It was February 1998 when I wheeled in with Zak.

With the builder finally finished, my carers and family came over and spent the weekend cleaning away the dirt and dust thickly layered on every surface. Then the removalists delivered the new furniture and appliances I had bought over the last few months.

With everything in place as much as it could be, Mum was the last to leave on the Sunday afternoon, leaving Zak and me alone.

Those first few hours felt unreal, like a dream. I was in my own house, with my own couch, my own TV and my own microwave. I was alone and it felt great, although Zak was a little put out that we weren't going back to my parents' place. I wheeled into each room, touching the walls to make sure it wasn't a dream, surveying where everything was to get a sense of orientation. I felt so free that if I had been able to, I would have stripped off and run around the house naked, screaming with excitement. Instead, I savoured the moment of being the lord of the manor and of my life.

The first night alone in the house, as I lay awake watching fine beams of light trace across the ceiling, reminded me of the first night I got myself out of my car and into bed. I felt pure contentment and satisfaction on achieving my goal.

My thirtieth birthday became a combined house-warming which turned into a very big night. It took me a week to recover from the dodgy cask wine, a friend vomited in the gutter, another pashed a neighbour up the road, and my next-door neighbour broke his arm jumping over the fence. It was vastly different from my twentieth birthday party on 14 July 1988, which I celebrated with a cake and jumper while lying in the ICU unable to breathe by myself, thinking my life was over. My thirtieth was a celebration of the last ten years with my family and friends from pre- and post-accident; my two lives had now come together. In a way it was my rebirth, the triumph of rebuilding my life. This was the moment I felt I'd finally caught up to where I should have been, albeit ten years late.

MY HOME

Moving away from my parents' secure nest changed me. I felt whole, confident and in control. The decisions I made were mine to own, and most of all I had physical and psychological freedom, my independence.

When I was in rehabilitation, all I'd hoped for—as with many others going through the spinal unit—was to be independent. I hoped to be able to do all the daily living tasks without relying on help—going to the toilet, getting dressed, preparing meals, getting into bed or going out.

The goal I had been working towards since my accident was to become as independent as possible. Being able to transfer by myself changed my life; however, by 1996, although I had expended vast amounts of energy relearning many of the daily tasks I had set for myself, some, such as showering below my waist and attending to my bowels, still eluded me. I eventually managed to work out a way to dress myself with jeans (no undies, they were too hard to get on), a T-shirt, jumper and runners (although I could never put on a shirt and tuck it in or knot a tie anyway). And I could even cook some simple but tasty meals, including chicken rogani, my specialty. However, if I was to do everything with minimal assistance from carers, it would take most of the day, leaving little time for anything else.

To be able to go to work so I could pay off a house and enlarge my personal freedom meant that I had to relinquish some independence, relying on carers to assist me more in the mornings. This sped up my morning routine from snail pace and allowed me to get up at a respectable 5 a.m. and be at work by 9 a.m. By sacrificing a little independence in one area, I could achieve the far greater goal of starting a new career.

Inevitably, moving into my house I needed more support from carers both in the morning and in the afternoon when I got home from work to help with cooking, cleaning, shopping, walking Zak and general tasks around the house. Living on my own was new and exciting; I loved hosting dinner parties, letting loose with friends without a worry—aside from the hangover the next day. Many of my new carers were young with a world of interests, and I quickly developed some close friendships.

Feeling less constrained, I became more open to other opportunities and the prospect of relationships began to feature on my mind. Although I had quadriplegia, I didn't feel any different or have any fewer wants or desires than when I was able-bodied. Our physical bodies are only part of us. Our minds determine who we are and how we feel. My mind wasn't broken, and I still wanted all the things I'd wanted previously—to be loved, to be found attractive, to want someone to want and desire me, and to be intimate with me.

I'd had a few passing relationships over the years but none of any real duration. It had been a 'long time between drinks,' and I felt like a teenager discovering girls for the first time: the excitement, anticipation, hormones in overdrive, and fantasies filling my mind at night.

My first long-term relationship after my accident happened when I moved out of home. My friendship with one of my carers—let's call her Mary—developed slowly into an intimate long-term relationship. I was attracted to her from the first time I met her at the interview. Dressed in a short black skirt, tight top and high heels, she was confident and compelling. She was twenty-seven, tall and curvy, with long dark hair. We connected immediately, and with her outgoing personality we were rarely stuck for conversation.

She began working for me when I moved into my house, doing a couple of afternoon shifts, helping me with walking Zak, household stuff such as cooking dinner, cleaning, washing, and so on, and she would come out with me to wheelchair rugby on a Wednesday night. We'd get back late, occasionally getting a few beers or ciders from the bottle-shop on the way home, and sit around talking late into the evening, getting to know one another. When I worked late, past the time her shift would finish, she'd meet me on my way home near her place and give me my cooked dinner in the car. I would look forward to seeing her on the next shift and when she gave me a cheeky smile, I had a fair idea there was something between us, although there was the forbidden professional line in the sand.

With my rising hormone and lust levels, I guess I reached a point where, whatever the consequences, I needed to know if there was anything between us. As she walked out the front door one night I wheeled up and said, 'Mary, before you go, can you come here?', gesturing her closer. 'Yeah, what, Dave?' she asked, leaning down through the doorway. Without hesitation I kissed her on the cheek. We both looked at each other in surprise—*what just happened?*—then I kissed her again, but this time on the lips. We knew we had crossed the line of no return, and our relationship heated up like a blast furnace from that moment on.

It was initially a very intense and exciting roller coaster of a relationship; we couldn't get enough of each other or, in my case, I couldn't stop thinking about her. It was wonderful being with someone completely different from anyone else I'd been with. Being in my own home and spending all morning in bed, or enjoying a lazy Sunday afternoon at a pub or bar seeing a jazzy/blues band with a few friends, was a new and exciting experience for me.

Although our relationship fizzled out much like it had started and was over within a year, it was the longest I had been with someone at the time. The experience, especially in the early intense stages, offered the first real opportunity of sexual self-discovery with my disability.

One bonus of having quadriplegia is that your reflex system is still intact, which enables you to get an erection. However, I would like to clarify that even with two people who have the same disability, there will be differences in how their bodies work, so I can speak only from my experience. Although the ability to get a hard-on was useful for attaching my condom drainage, it didn't last long which was a bit of a bugger when it came to sex. It was great at the start but after a few minutes, it slowly deflated like a hose when the water is shut off.

At the time, to get a long-lasting erection some people used what was known as an 'erection injection,' a drug injected into the penis. A nurse friend said long-term use can damage the blood vessels so I never gave it a go but, then again, I didn't need to at the time.

One guy told me about his experience with the 'erection injection' and I discovered it wasn't an exact science. Fifteen minutes after the doctor injected the drug, he was the proud owner of a damn-good stiffy. 'It will wear off in an hour or two,' the doctor assured him.

Four hours later, with a cucumber-sized member in his tracksuit, he had to deliver a talk to a group of schoolkids. The only way to hide it was to put his man-bag (that held wallet, keys, etc.) on his lap. The doctor ended up draining the blood from his old fella to get it down. Evidently, the dosage was a little hit or miss.

The introduction of Viagra that year revolutionised sex and experimentation for people like me with erectile issues. Drop a pill and the 'wood' would last for hours. While being stimulated it is up; stop the stimulation, it goes back down. This meant I could take a pill in the afternoon and be a sex machine that night or the next morning. It gave me and my partner much more freedom, flexibility and, best of all, a little more spontaneity.

However, one drawback was the lack of control in the morning with the carers. The slightest movement, or droplets of water from the shower, gave it a mind of its own and despite willing it to behave, it had no effect. Particularly with male carers, it was extremely hard not to be self-conscious about having an uncontrollable erection, with the pinnacle of embarrassment being when they had to bend my erect member like a stiff tent pole to connect the condom to the leg-bag tube, neatly forming a super structure in my undies.

For me now, sex is not just about the physical act. It has become much more than what it used to be: it is sex with the mind. There is still the physical side, much of which can be experienced with a bit of ingenuity and limited only by a person's imagination. I have some sensation so I can feel certain areas, but it's far from normal and I don't ejaculate, but this differs greatly with each person. The bits of sensation I still have can be enhanced by concentrating and focusing on each sense and feeling. But the most enjoyable and satisfying aspect is being in the moment with my partner. Learning about her, understanding what she likes and dislikes, the closeness, the touch, the taste, sharing ideas, fears and dreams. The physical is only one small part; it's the psychological intensity and connection that is satisfying—the mind fuck.

29

MOVING FORWARD

I had changed my old 'glasses' for new ones; the world now looked so different since the lonely nights I'd lain awake in Ward 17, trying to imagine my future. I now had many more opportunities than I could ever have imagined.

With opportunity came decisions. *Where do I want my life to head?* I asked myself. It was exciting to have this choice and be in control of my destiny.

I was working long hours as a design draftsman in the building service division at Connell Wagner. The long hours were usually due to tight deadlines which I'm sure were imposed to restrict our time designing, thereby saving money; however, it just meant that I spent more time working after hours. I had come to realise that I needed a challenge, something to get me out of bed in the morning. I needed to have a plan, a goal, and be moving forward with purpose, otherwise I felt I was stagnating. I was getting bored with the job and needed a change.

I was fortunate to have the opportunity to work with Graham in the fire services area doing design, but also some project management, installing fire protection systems in government housing and nursing homes. This allowed me to go onsite, which I loved, instead of being stuck in the office. Most of the places had reasonable wheelchair access where I could usually get myself around. They were only small projects, but being thrown into the deep end gave me a small taste of what project management was about. This was the impetus I needed to give me a direction and motivation for where to head in my career.

I was still fitting wheelchair rugby into my week, playing at the local competition and using up most of my annual leave to compete at the National Games and other tournaments. But then I enrolled to study part-time at Victoria University, doing a graduate diploma in project management, and this, combined with working full-time, ate away all my spare time for the next four years. I had to stop playing wheelchair rugby.

Moving into the project management division at Connell Wagner was a steep learning curve, and stressful at times as I tried to manage contractors, designers and the clients to achieve a common goal. There are many skills, methodologies and knowledge required to be a good project manager, but to save you the excruciating boredom of me rambling on about it, one of the most important aspects is planning. In project management we refer to it as the 3 Ps: Piss Poor Planning = Piss Poor Performance.

One positive side to acquiring a disability is that you generally become a good planner. I guess that is one reason I am drawn to project management; the other is, I like telling people what to do.

From the time I get up to when I go to bed, I plan. I plan to get up at a set time, I plan resources (carers), I plan when to go to the toilet, I plan for varying weather conditions, I plan for potential obstacles, such as going to an unknown location; in short, I plan for everything.

Speaking of unknown locations: my first date with Michelle, an English girl I met at a work colleague's grand final BBQ in 2001, became one of my many monumental logistics exercises. We had planned to meet at a bar near my work, but I hadn't been there before. The planning process began with me calling up to confirm that the venue was wheelchair accessible, including the toilets. 'Yes, and it has a handrail!' said the bubbly voice through the phone.

I took her word for it. Doing a little upfront reconnaissance by driving past the venue, I identified that the carpark at the front was on too much of a slope. However, down the road there was a suitable place for me to park and get out of the car, but it was a long push to the venue. I figured I would have to leave more time to push up to the bar: this was the contingency. Although the gradient on the path up to the venue wasn't too steep, the ramp into the bar was more than I could handle, so I planned to arrive even earlier to get a staff member to push me up.

First dates are about first impressions. Once I did get there, I had to plan what to eat so it didn't end in embarrassment with part of my meal shooting off the plate into my lap as I tried to cut it up—but that's another story.

The date ended up going very well, and Michelle and I were together for the next three years. As a footnote: Michelle discovered I couldn't get up the ramp when I had to go outside into the street to empty my leg-bag. The toilet, as it turned out, was not wheelchair accessible. But there was a handrail!

I had proven myself at Connell Wagner and people were aware of my capabilities, but there were times when, upon meeting a person for the first time, he or she would see the wheelchair rather than me.

Some years after I started a secondment position at Melbourne Water, I was told that when my name was put up to a certain manager for a three-month secondment role, he was concerned whether I could do the job as I was in a wheelchair. My manager at Connell Wagner assured the person that I would be fine and if it didn't work out I could be easily moved on. I ended up being seconded for four years, then I was offered a permanent position where I stayed for over seven years, taking on various roles.

Melbourne Water was a great organisation to work for with many fantastic people who made it what it was. They were always very supportive of my needs and would do whatever was necessary to enable me to do my job. But my point here is that even though some people may have been sceptical, their doubts were negated by action—by me showing them what I could do. One may say this is discrimination, but the reality is that some people have little understanding of disability, and some even find it a bit scary. As I see it, part of my responsibility is to help educate the community so that when the next person with a disability comes along, he or she will hopefully get an easier ride.

There were certainly times when I wondered how I would deal with a situation, in particular, wheelchair access on a project; but with planning, most obstacles could be overcome or I would get the job done another way.

For example, it was only later, when working at Melbourne Water, that I came up against access challenges due to the locations of the work. My projects ranged from small $50k pump-motor replacements to complex multi-million-dollar plant rectifications or upgrades to treat water for drinking or sewerage. In general, many work locations were in non-wheelchair-friendly areas.

If it was somewhere I hadn't been before, I'd make a few preliminary phone calls to check out access. If there were steps or it was difficult to get around, I would try to meet an operator onsite or bring a colleague from the office to help. This was fine most of the time, providing I gave clear instructions.

One warm spring day I was inspecting a small water treatment plant at Pakenham, located in the middle of a green grassed paddock with cows roaming the landscape and a gravel track cutting through for access from the main road. I was with about ten consultants and a colleague from the office, Ellia. We were at the bottom of a small hill on the access track while I gave them the run-through of the project to tender for the design works' package.

'Ellia, can you give me a hand up the hill?' I asked as I finished my conversation with a consultant. Before the last word passed my lips, Ellia grabbed my wheelchair and suddenly pulled it back. Time stopped as I flipped forward, with the sensation of being stationary in mid-air, before I plunged back to earth. *Whack!* My body slapped onto the gravel track like a slab of meat thrown onto a butcher's block. As I lay sprawled on the ground, my dark-blue suit pants and mauve shirt covered in dirt, the bewildered consultants just stared at me. My head was pounding from landing on it, and I felt so embarrassed I wanted to crawl into the ant hole beside me and hide.

After some very clear directions, Ellia and one of the consultants lifted me into my chair and I continued with the meeting. I was still picking stones out of my scalp two days later. My learning: clearer communication was needed.

But much of the time I didn't have the luxury of an Ellia and relied on getting myself around. If that wasn't possible, I could always find someone to take photos onsite and I'd review them at the office.

I got to know most of the contractors on the projects quite well and built good relationships with many of them over time—and they became accepting and willing to help me get around. However, there were occasions when I came to a site to inspect the work, and things quickly became uncomfortable.

One of my projects was to install new one-tonne concrete anchor blocks and retaining chains to hold floating aerators in position in a sewerage pond. The site was difficult for me, and I struggled to push over the grass and dirt track, so I got the contractor to give me a shove around the perimeter of a pond full of sewerage, keeping an eye on the sloping edge so as not to roll in.

During my inspection, I discovered that they had used the wrong material on the chains and told them they would need replacing. This was going to cost a lot as divers would have to go into the ponds and replace them. The contractor was fuming, arguing with me to get me to change my mind. I couldn't and wouldn't budge on my decision. As he pushed me back over the rough, inaccessible terrain, the air was thick with tension. I could almost hear his teeth grinding. 'Miserable prick' was his 'friendly' good-bye.

30

THE SEED

As mentioned, Michelle wasn't put off by my inability to get back up the ramp at the bar, nor the night within the first few weeks of sleeping together when I shat the bed—with her in it. I don't know if it was the chicken and vegetable stir-fry with a tripling of oyster sauce, but around midnight I awoke in a daze thinking I had just expelled a big fart. As a waft of hot pungent smell rose to the top of the doona, I realised *that was not a fart!* Reaching behind me, I felt something hot and soft, making me suddenly panic.

'Michelle, Michelle!' I yelped.

'Yeah, what, Dave?' she asked, sleepily, rolling towards me.

'I ... I think I've crapped myself!' The length of the pause made me think she hadn't heard me, and I was about to say it again when she said in her gentle English accent, 'Oh yeah, I think you have.'

The crime scene was horrible, and as I dragged myself across the bed to get onto the commode, I made it far worse by leaving a huge skid-mark from one side of the bed to the other. But to her credit, Michelle took it in her stride and without gagging, helped me out of bed and into the shower, then remade the bed.

'Shit happens, ay!' I joked, trying to lighten the experience.

'I've had worse with Sarah,' she said.

Michelle was divorced and had Sarah, her seven-year-old

daughter, half the time. When she wasn't with Sarah, she was at my place, as it was more wheelchair-accessible than hers and I needed my carers in the morning. Some nights after work I'd drop by her place, but it was important that she had her time with Sarah, and the arrangement worked well for both of us as I enjoyed some time alone.

Michelle was slim, with dark-brown shoulder-length hair framing her fine attractive features. She had a strong physique developed through her teens doing gymnastics (which enabled her to get me and my chair up a few stairs) and was a genuine and warm person. I had met her through some common friends whom we'd see at the usual events like the footy grand final, Melbourne Cup, St Patrick's Day, or for any excuse really. Many of her friends were English and Irish, so it would often end up a fairly big night. 'Goin oome already? Don't be a fooken eejit. Coome and ave anoother drink, the noites still yoong!' was the typical response to those trying to get away at a respectable time.

Our daily lives moved along; I had recently moved into project management at Connell Wagner and was enjoying the work. My main focus was on progressing my career, while Michelle was studying.

I felt content being with her: she was calm and easy to be with. And being English, she didn't mind a glass of wine, which she called 'bottled sunshine.' Dinner parties at her place were full of conversation and laughter enhanced by the amount of 'sunshine' consumed.

Occasionally we'd get away for a night on a weekend, taking a drive up to the Murray River in northern Victoria or down the coast. So that I could get by without a carer, I would plan it so I didn't need to go to the toilet while we were away, and Michelle would only have to help me with showering and getting dressed, with which I was more comfortable.

We had talked about our future, and even considered moving in together, but that was as far as we got. It wasn't one thing, but an accumulation of many that took the gloss off the idea. There were the limitations of Michelle's situation that weren't congruent with my desire to move north to a warmer climate; but also, the idea of buying a bigger house that would require a new mortgage filled me with dread. I had already made so many sacrifices to pay off my house, putting off many things that were important to me like travelling overseas, going on interstate holidays or being in a position to try new things, such as going to a nice restaurant. The idea of having another mortgage didn't interest me at all.

When Michelle came over one night and said, 'I'm going to visit my brother in Italy this July,' without inviting me to come, I felt hurt and disappointed. When I first met her, I was planning to go to Europe with some of my family members, but being lust-struck, I decided to pass on the opportunity to visit Spain and France as I thought I'd go with Michelle in the near future. Now she was going without me.

'OK, well, I'm going skiing for a couple of weeks then,' I said. It was the best I could do on such short notice, not wanting her to know I was really annoyed. I had tried snow-skiing while at the TAC Rehab Centre in 1989, but with little arm strength and a very heavy sit-ski which I could barely control, as well as being unable to deal with the cold and having other priorities at the time, I didn't pursue it. But in 2003, I decided to have another go, by which stage lighter and more advanced equipment had become available. The sit-ski consists of a frame that you sit in, with your feet out in front, propped on top of two skis. I also had outriggers (little skis) strapped to my hands to provide balance. To control the speed and direction of the sit-ski I would lean slightly with my head and arms, and do big sweeping turns. With the assistance of a ski guide, I was eventually able get myself down beginner runs without crashing. It was the best fun!

When Michelle got back, it wasn't long before the relationship went completely downhill with Michelle breaking it off. I wasn't surprised: I had expected it and, in a way, felt relieved.

We'd had a fun, caring and enjoyable relationship while it lasted but, in the end, we weren't heading down the same path and we wanted different things. My only regret, which was of my doing, was that I missed out on going to Europe with my family.

This brought home to me that missed opportunities might not come again. I didn't want to get to the end of my life wishing I had taken the opportunity to do things when I had the chance. I don't think it was a midlife crisis—I was only thirty-six—but more a realisation that life races by so quickly.

I felt acutely that it was now time for me to step beyond my immediate challenges and seek out other experiences, pushing myself further, stepping outside my comfort zone and into the unknown, in pursuit of a long-lost dream.

I had been to almost every Australian International Airshow at Avalon since it started in 1992. In summer, Avalon airfield is a hot, windy, dry, dusty paddock unless it rains; then it becomes a cold, windy, wet, muddy paddock. With the old war birds roaring past and the latest fighter jets screaming through their spectacular manoeuvres, it's pure testosterone in the sky.

A tiny spark still flickered inside me, keeping alive my boyhood dream to fly, despite Mrs Corcoran in Year 7 telling me I would never be a pilot with my grades. All my life, whenever I heard a plane overhead, I couldn't help but look up. I'm drawn skywards with an incredible urge. Growing up I was mad on planes. Pete and I would put two chairs side by side on the patio, set up some plyboards in front of the chairs and draw instruments on them in chalk. I would invariably demand to be the captain and Pete my co-pilot. We would sit for hours re-enacting the Battle of Britain, pretending to shoot down the Gerries. 'Blue Leader, this is Red Leader. Gerries at five o'clock. Dive, dive, dive!' I'd imitate as the characters from the movie played in my imagination.

When I was around twelve or thirteen years old, I saw a documentary of two army ultralight pilots flying across Australia. God, I so much wanted to be them. I promised myself that one day when I had the money, I would learn to fly.

At the 2005 airshow I came across a display by the Southern Microlight club. In its full glory, the most amazing flying machine I had ever seen was urging me to come over. It was a Microlight Trike. A Microlight Trike is basically a powered hang glider. I loved the idea of gliding like a bird and having the power to go places. But what attracted me in particular was the simplicity. The trike is constructed of a large hang-glider wing, with a pod hanging below the wing like a pendulum where the pilot and passenger sit (the pilot at the front between the passenger's legs). The motor is on the back, with a front and two rear wheels so it takes off and lands like a plane.

To control it in flight, there is a horizontal bar called the base-bar which hangs in front of the pilot and is connected to the wing. To steer, you push the base-bar left or right, which shifts the weight of the pod, causing the aircraft to turn—which is why they are called Weight Shift Microlights. To make it climb and descend, the pilot powers the engine up and down. Very simple!

Rapid-firing questions in my eagerness to Barry and Michael, the pilots from the Southern Microlight Club, I asked, 'I don't have a lot of strength, how hard is it to fly?'

'I can fly it with one finger,' said Barry.

I was hooked, like a bogan to Bundy and Coke. I had to do it. Unlike other aircraft that require good hand and finger function to use the controls, this required only gross arm movements which I thought I could do. Hell yeah, this was it.

I had never given the idea of flying much thought following my accident, as it had seemed so far from being a possibility. But when I saw the trike, I saw the possibilities, not the obstacles.

In Easter that year, I was staying at the Able Management Group (AMG) in Harrietville near Bright in Victoria, a wheelchair-accessible rustic cottage with disabled facilities, set on a couple of acres on the banks of the Ovens River. The AMG is a not-for-profit organisation that gets people with disabilities back into sport and activities. The AMG helped me get back into snow skiing in 2004, by providing equipment such as a Bi-Unique sit-ski and volunteer ski guides. The ski guides helped me on the mountain, sitting me back up when I inevitably crashed, lifting me on and off the chairlifts, or helping me stop before I took out an out-of-control snowboarder.

I was telling Nick, one of the founders and camp managers, about the trike. He handed me a brochure that showed a trike flying over Mt Buffalo. *Eagle School of Microlighting, Trial Instructional Flights over Bright*, it read.

'Give Steve Ruffels a call,' Nick suggested.

The next day was perfect, blue sky and no wind with a slight chill in the air. Steve was buzzing around like a bushfly sorting out passengers for the next Trial Instructional Flight (TIF), one being me. Lisa, Steve's wife, who was also an instructor, was taking up passengers in their second trike.

'The temperature drops by three degrees for every thousand feet; it will be pretty cold at five thousand feet. You'd better get a jacket,' Steve said, pointing to the wall lined with coats.

I did a quick calculation: *that's close to zero. Yep, better wear a jacket.* Nick and Emily, my carer, lifted me into the back seat of the trike and strapped me in. A mixture of excitement and nerves coursed through my body as Steve rearranged my feet so they wouldn't get jammed in the foot controls used to steer on the ground.

Steve sat between my legs; I was sitting quite high behind him which made me feel a little unstable, but I wasn't going anywhere with the waist and shoulder straps on. Kicking the engine over, the two-stroke coughed to life, vibrating like an unbalanced washing machine on spin cycle.

'Hold the wing while I taxi,' Steve said, pointing where to put my hands on the training bars out to the side within easy reach, as we bumped along the grass runway.

Stopping at the end, Steve said, 'OK Dave, to turn left you push this bar to the right, to go right you push it the other way. To make it fly faster, pull the bar towards you and to fly slower, push it away. Got that?'

'Yup,' I said, my heart racing.

Turning onto the runway, Steve opened the throttle full, the engine screaming. The acceleration pushed me back in the seat as we rapidly picked up speed. I looked down, the ground suddenly dropped away, and we shot up to the heavens like a rocket. I gasped with the exhilaration. *This is unbelievable, woohoo!* I thought as we climbed higher and higher, the valley opening up in the distance.

Levelling out, the excitement was replaced by the gentleness of the flight with the earth slowly moving below, the maze of mountains and valleys stretching into the blue horizon. I was surprised that I could smell eucalyptus wafting up from the trees below with the rising heat of the morning sun. Although the bright sun warmed my face through my visor, the chill of the icy wind nibbled at the exposed skin around my neck, reminding me of how high we must be as we headed over Mt Buffalo, the trike buffeted by the thermals developing off the huge wall of granite.

'Put your hands up here and do some turns,' said Steve.

I reached for the training bars but without triceps, the force of the wind kept pushing my hands away.

'I can't hold the bar, Steve!' I yelled through the intercom.

He grabbed my hands and wrapped my fingers around the training bars, holding them closed so I could get the feel of flying.

All too soon, Steve cut the engine over Mt Buffalo and we circled over the airfield, losing height with each turn, before greasing in for a smooth landing. I was hooked. I had to do it. What a buzz!

'Do you know of anyone with quadriplegia who has flown?' I asked excitedly.

'I've heard of some paraplegics, but not quadriplegics,' Steve said as he rubbed his chin thoughtfully.

'Do you think it would be possible for someone with my disability to fly it?' I asked, feeling hopeful.

'Well, with some modifications it might be possible; it's pretty simple to fly. Maybe you could rig up some hand clamps or something,' Steve suggested.

'Might be possible' were the magic words. They were all I needed to sow the seed.

31

DISAPPOINTMENT

As soon as I got home, I searched the internet for an instructor near Melbourne. Jim's availability was restricted to weekends and, waiting for the right conditions, it took a few agonising weeks before we could do a trial flight.

Vinny, the first person with paraplegia to sail nonstop around the world, was at the airfield when I arrived, being trained by Jim, and had recently completed his first solo. I was intrigued by the modifications to his aircraft, using a go-cart seat for support and twist grips on the base-bar to steer the front wheel—not that they would be any use to me with my hands.

It was a typical Melbourne morning, grey overcast sky with a gentle breeze. Dad came down to help me get in, along with Gaz, my carer. With the trike being quite high off the ground, the two of them lifted me into the front seat, which had a small backrest and lap seat belt to hold me in.

My feet had to be arranged just right to sit on the foot supports without getting caught on the brake or throttle pedal. 'Put my foot on the foot post. All the way on, no, too far forward. Yeah, bring it back. No, too far, more forward, that's it!' I instructed.

Using duct tape, Gaz taped my hands to the horizontal base-bar in front of me as I couldn't hold it without finger function.

Sporting my red ski jacket, sitting in the front seat of the trike, an open cockpit with no sides, I waited for Jim to put on his warm freezer suit. Unexpectedly, a gust of wind grabbed the huge wing, pushing one side down like an umbrella at the beach. With the base-bar attached to me, it pulled me over to the side, then back the other way, flopping me over like a rag doll.

A chilling thought popped into my mind. Like a rolling film sequence, I imagined taking off, hitting turbulence, and without any balance, falling to the side with my hands still attached to the base-bar, my bum slipping off the seat, while the spectators on the ground viewed a body dangling out the side of the aircraft. 'I think I need a chest strap!' I announced, prompting Dad to rush to the car to see what could be used to tie around me.

Taxiing out to Runway 22, I was filled with a mixture of nervous anticipation and intense excitement: I was about to realise my dream to fly. I had thought about flying constantly, playing it over and over in my mind thousands of times, visualising what it would be like. I was so sure I would be able to do it. This was my moment.

At full throttle, with the engine screaming, the small aircraft shot into the air, climbing at such a steep angle it felt like we were going to tip backwards. We bounced through a few small spots of turbulence, with my bum still in the seat, the pod dangling off the wing like a pendulum and my taped hands going with the motion of the base-bar as it jolted left and right. Climbing higher into the smooth air, at 2500 feet we levelled out. Over the intercom Jim said, 'OK, make a turn to the right.'

'OK,' I said.

Unsure how far to go or how much force to use, I pushed the bar a little to the left. I was surprised how much heavier the wing felt in the air; I was not sure how Barry could fly with one finger.

'OK, turn to the left,' said Jim.

Gathering all my strength, again I pushed on the bar, slowly moving it to the right, the trike banking into a slow left turn.

'OK, straighten up,' he said. On command, I pushed the bar back around to level flight.

'We'll go back down now,' Jim said, his voice muffled with the sound of rushing wind and the chime of the 582 Rotax engine.

'Oh … OK?' I said, thinking it was a little short. I figured that I'd be doing a few more turns to try to get the hang of it.

Jim wrenched the bar over, rolling the aircraft to the left like an obedient Brumby. Lining up on Runway 22, the trike bounced around in the gentle turbulence and Jim effortlessly snapped the bar left and right to keep it on approach. The slow motion of the world changed to a rushing river of green as the ground raced up. Jim pushed the base-bar forward, fully stretching out my taped arms, to 'flare' just before touchdown.

Slowly, Jim taxied us back to the hangar, stopping on the grass just before an open stormwater drain, then shut down the engine.

'What do you think?' I asked in hope, unsure what his answer would be.

'I don't think you will be able to fly a trike, you don't have enough strength,' Jim said as he unclipped himself from the back seat. 'Maybe you should try something else.'

As his words sank in, my spirit drained from my body, I felt absolutely crushed. I hadn't thought of anything except flying a trike for the last few months. I didn't want to fly anything else; it was my dream, my destiny, my sole purpose in life at that moment. I was so sure I could do it.

The rest of the conversation was a blur; it didn't matter anymore, my dream of flying was over. Wheeling to the car, I saw Vinny and John, another student, working through an exam in the hangar while Jim attended to other TIF customers. I couldn't help but feel envious and bitterly disappointed.

32

HOPE

A little seed was always sitting in the back of my mind, waiting for the right conditions to crack its hard shell and spring to life.

Some weeks later, after our usual Sunday roast dinner at my parents' place, I was chatting with my sister EJ about what had happened with the instructor and the disappointment of losing my dream. Maybe I just needed someone to believe in me, to re-spark a little hope, I really don't know. But her simple words, 'You'll work out a way, you always do,' suddenly shifted something inside me.

With those words, that tiny seed sprouted. The next day I went out for a push around my local streets; it's a good way to clear my head and think. I began to feel that I could see a little clearer. It was as if someone had flicked on a light switch, and now I could see the way out. I could again see the possibilities, not the impossibilities.

Thinking through each step of the flying experience with Jim, I realised that having my hands positioned on the base-bar with my palms facing down gave me little strength to push the bar sideways. Holding my hands in a vertical position would give me much more power because I could pull and use my biceps. The solution was so simple, I was sure it would work.

To confirm my hypothesis, I needed to make an adaptation that could bolt onto the base-bar of the trike to hold my hands in the vertical position, and then have another go. Duncan, a friend I had met through my project management work who was an engineer and inventor, offered his help.

'Dave, you design it, I will build it,' he said.

I called Jim to tell him my brilliant idea and asked whether I could come down to take some measurements off his trike for my adaptation. He accommodated me, but I felt that he was just going along with it, maybe hoping I would lose interest. Unfortunately for him, I was like a dog with a bone. My energy and determination were back; I wasn't going to let it go until I had exhausted all possibilities.

The base-bar adaptation was only one part of the solution. I needed to build up my strength to give myself the best chance. The few working muscles I had left had to be trained and strengthened using the same movements as in flying.

Dad helped me develop my trike 'flight simulator.' Outside under the pergola we installed a rod that hung from a beam and supported a long rectangular wooden box that Dad made, with a slot at each end into which to place my hands. Bungee straps were connected from the ends of the box to the pergola posts for resistance. Each night after work and at weekends, I pushed the box back and forth, over and over again until I was spent, sores developing on my wrists from the constant rubbing of my skin on the wood. Initially I could only do a dozen reps, but over the next four months I slowly got stronger, eventually building up to one hundred repetitions, then increasing the load by adding more bungee straps, then starting over again.

Training in the cold winter evenings was hard and I found it difficult to keep motivated. I had to force myself to get out each time, especially when I'd had a hard day at work. It was so easy to make an excuse not to do it. But when I felt my motivation waning, I took a moment to look at a cool picture of a trike banking sharply into a turn stuck to a wall in my study to remind myself why I was doing it—my dream to fly.

As soon as I had completed my design, Duncan got to work and built my hand adaptation. It looked a little agricultural, but it would do the job.

By early September 2005 I was feeling good; I was stronger, my adaptation was complete, all I needed was to try it out and see if I could realise my dream. I was hoping Jim would be impressed by my enthusiasm and ingenuity and give me another go.

I rang him up. 'Jim, I've finished that adaptation I spoke to you about and was hoping to try it out. Just wondering if I could put it on your trike and go up with you, just to see?'

'Mmm, I'm not sure. I haven't seen it and I don't want to damage the aircraft,' he said.

'It just bolts on to the base-bar, it won't damage it,' I insisted.

'You need a fair amount of strength to pull the bar around; I really don't think you will be able to do it,' he said.

'I've been training for months building up my strength, and I reckon the hand adaption will work because it holds my hands differently. I have more strength now,' I said with desperation.

'The weather isn't too good at this time of year. I don't know when I will be going down next.'

'Can I call you next weekend and see if it's suitable?'

'Yeah, OK,' he said.

The following week I checked the weather, thinking it looked OK with relatively light wind and no rain.

'Hi Jim, it's Dave again. Just wondering if you were going down?'

'No, the conditions aren't right,' he said.

The following week was the same, as was the next, the next and the next. Finally, he had to go down to the airfield to take another guy up, so what could he say?

Bolting my adaptation on only took a couple of minutes to make it secure. Strapped in, I sat my feet onto the foot pegs like last time, trying to avoid the throttle and brake pedals. This time I wasn't nervous but filled with excited anticipation of what might be.

Starting up, we taxied a couple of metres, then Jim shut the engine down.

'Something's wrong,' he said.

He checked a few things, I checked my feet, they seemed OK, and he started the engine again. Throttling up, we moved another couple of metres, then he shut the engine off again.

'This isn't going to work,' he said.

He got out. It was over.

33

WHO WILL HELP ME?

All I wanted was a chance to give it a go. If it didn't work then fine, I could live with that. My frustration soon turned into dejection as I could not find another instructor close to Melbourne. Hearing that other people had their doubts didn't help my confidence or my hope of finding a willing instructor.

I thought I might be in luck when someone mentioned Tony who trained out of Benalla, about two-and-a-half hours away. But my hope quickly evaporated after talking to Teresa, Tony's wife, who said he had stopped training students. The only other person she knew of who might consider giving me a go was Steve Ruffels at Eagle School of Microlighting in Bright, over a four-hour drive from Melbourne. I had taken my initial trial instructional flight with Steve the previous Easter, and he seemed like a nice enough guy and fairly positive. But I wasn't sure how long this would last once I asked him to give me a go.

I was worried because, as far as I knew, he was pretty much my last chance, short of travelling interstate which would have been so much more difficult, and even then I had no idea whether I would find someone willing to help me.

I nervously rang Steve; he was at the supermarket buying milk. 'Steve, it's Dave Jacka here. I'm not sure if you remember me but I'm the guy in the wheelchair, the quadriplegic you took up for a TIF last Easter.'

A brief pause. 'Ah yes, I remember you.'

After explaining my situation and that I had developed my base-bar adaptation, I nervously asked, 'I was wondering if you'd be willing to take me up and give me a go?'

My heart was in my mouth waiting for his answer.

'I can't see it being a problem. When can you get here?'

After a moment of stunned silence, I said, 'Ah, ah… this weekend?

'OK, see you then. We'll start doing the theory too.'

I hung up the phone and gathered my thoughts. *Shit!*

Dad and I left Friday night, driving up to Bright in the pouring rain. Halfway there, Steve called to say it would be raining all weekend but there might be some breaks where we could fly and start the theory. I heard Lisa in the background saying something like, 'It's not worth coming up, it will be raining all weekend.' Steve thought about it for a moment and then agreed with her.

'Let's organise another weekend so we can make sure we get you up for a fly,' he said.

Although I didn't get to Bright that weekend, I wasn't too disappointed. Firstly, when I got back home, I came down with a bad dose of the flu which knocked me out for four days; the cancellation was a blessing in disguise. More importantly, this conversation was my first glimpse of Steve's optimism: even with a lot of uncertainty, he was willing to give it a go and see what happened.

A few weeks later was the Melbourne Cup weekend, 2005, my next opportunity to fly. It was a demonstration event for Airborne microlights at the Porepunkah airfield, hosted by the Eagle School of Microlighting. It was humid and wet with periods of rain. Still, a lot of people came out to look at and try the different Airborne trikes under instruction. I had planned to stay for four days in the hope that, if I did succeed, I would get as much airtime in as possible and start my theory.

I arrived at the airfield Saturday morning on 29 October 2005 and waited in the hangar with other wannabe pilots, hoping for a break in the weather.

'Oh shit,' I mouthed, as Jim walked past. I was momentarily in shock. With my paranoia in overdrive, I feared the worst. I just hoped he wouldn't tell Steve I'd gone up with him and failed.

The weather started to clear in the late morning, and Steve took the growing line of people up for flights around Bright while I waited for my turn. It was getting late and I began to think that I wouldn't get a go.

'OK, Dave, you're next, let's get your bar adaptation on,' said Steve, busy doing ten things at once.

'Oh, OK,' I said, suddenly very alert, my stomach tightening.

Dad attached my bar, getting it in the right position, and with Emily, my carer, I was loaded into the front seat. This time I put my feet on the floor away from the foot posts and throttle and brake pedal so there wouldn't be any excuses.

I slid my gloved hands into my base-bar adaptation, locking them in firmly, and had a go at pulling the wing left, right, pushing it forward and backwards; it felt really good. Steve taxied up the side of the runway as he did last Easter, but this time it was very different. All the training and effort to develop the adaptation, the challenges and finding Steve had come together. I knew this was where I should be.

Going through the pre-flight checks, Steve said, 'When we throttle up, hold the wing level, push the bar all the way forward, holding it until we take off, then quickly pull it back towards you.'

'OK, got it,' I answered.

I didn't realise I would be taking off. Steve would steer the front nose-wheel and control the throttle.

'Hold the bar forward and level,' came Steve's muffled voice through the intercom, just audible over the wailing Rotax pushing us down the wet grass strip. It was hard to hold but I was managing, hoping to be off the ground quickly. The glue holding us to the earth suddenly came unstuck. We leapt into the air and I quickly pulled the bar back as Steve had instructed. As we climbed higher, my heart raced as we rocketed towards the low cloud base hanging around the tops of the mountains surrounding the valley.

My mind was in information overload; it took me a moment to realise: *I am flying!* Taking a deep breath, I relaxed a little and moved the base-bar, getting a feel for the aircraft. It was totally different with my adaptation, and it wasn't anywhere near as hard as before; it worked!

'Dave, turn to the left 180 degrees then to the right 180 and fly straight.'

'OK, but how steep?' I asked, as I pushed the bar over, further, then further again.

'That's a 30-degree turn, keep it there,' said Steve.

Completing the turn, I dragged the bar over, banking to the right with confidence, straightened up and flew straight. I continued flying around for thirty minutes, doing turns and following the road leading to Myrtleford from Bright.

With the airstrip dead ahead, I kept it straight and level, lining up the aircraft as we came in for landing, Steve reducing the throttle to make the aircraft descend. At fifty feet, he took over, using the training bars out to the side, finishing with a perfect smooth landing.

'You will be able to do landings like that,' he remarked.

'I hope so,' I answered with a huge smile on my face, ecstatic with how it went and Steve's generous encouragement.

That night I was on a high. I was booked in for the Monday and Tuesday to fly each morning and afternoon, and do a little theory in between. I wanted to know by the end of the weekend whether I would be capable of getting my pilot's certificate.

The weather improved over the next three days, getting warmer, and the skies cleared of rain. My confidence grew rapidly as I started to understand and feel the aircraft; Steve put me through the paces with 360-degree turns, figure eights, following the ridge line of mountains, landing approaches, and flying in various weather conditions.

On the third day, I sat parked in front of the IGA supermarket in Bright, enjoying the Monday afternoon sun with my window down, waiting for Emily to get some supplies. I was deep in thought, wondering whether Steve thought I would be able to progress to pilot. It was all I could think about.

Steve drove in, parked beside me and got out.

'Oh, hi Steve!' I said, surprised.

'Hi Dave,' Steve said. After a long pause, scratching his head, he said, 'Um, I was thinking about your flying.'

Oh, here it comes.

'You've progressed as fast as any of my other students, and I think you've gone as far as you can with your bar. I reckon the next step is to modify an aircraft so you can do everything else.'

'So, do you think I will be able to get my pilot's certificate?' I asked.

'With some modifications, I can't see why not.'

'Will you sell me one of your trikes then?' I excitedly shot back.

Whatever it cost, I didn't care. I knew I would now do it. My dream to fly was becoming a reality.

34

SOLO

I was totally focused. I ate, slept and breathed my dream of flying. With Steve on my side, no obstacle would be big enough to stop me.

Mid-November, Steve delivered my 'new' second-hand Edge X 582 trike with a Wizard Wing (a slow but very forgiving wing) to Aussie Adaptions for modification. I worked with them to develop the throttle control using push buttons, and to steer the front nose-wheel when on the ground by developing a hand-lever on my left-hand side—push it forward and the aircraft turns left, pull back and it turns right.

I took Vinny's idea of using a fibreglass go-cart seat for the pilot seat, as it provided greater lateral support so I didn't fall over and repositioned the magneto switches so I could use them without finger function.

I also designed a new improved base-bar adaptation incorporating push buttons for throttle control, but this time I used a roll cage manufacturer to construct it, as it had to have the highest quality welds and be certified.

I continued my fitness training on my simulator at home, and ravenously studied my theory. Mid-January I went back up to Bright for three days' additional flying training to reinforce my new skills while I waited for the modifications to be completed.

The ground steering would be the biggest challenge to get used to, so when Aussie Adaptations had completed their work, Dad and I took the trike (excluding the wing) to Tyabb airfield to test it out. It was a very hot day, in the mid-30s, and I was feeling the heat. The plan was for me to steer the trike with the new hand-lever from the front while Dad sat in the back, controlling the engine using my new throttle control.

I started the engine, Dad on the throttle gave it a bit of power, and the trike rolled slowly across the field. I practised a few turns and the steering lever worked quite well. The difficult part was getting used to which way to push or pull the lever to turn left or right, as it was counterintuitive. Midway downfield we hit a soft bit of ground; the trike came to an abrupt stop.

The throttle control didn't work like an accelerator on a car, decelerating when you took your foot off the pedal. The two push buttons drove an electric linear actuator that pulled and pushed the throttle cable, locking it in position until you pressed the alternate button to drive the actuator the opposite way, which took a couple of seconds.

'Give it a bit more throttle,' I said.

Dad pushed the revs up to 2500—still it didn't budge.

'Another thousand revs,' I said.

'Shiiiiiiiiiiiiiiiit!' I screamed as the trike broke loose, racing across the field, my vision blurred from the vibrations as we rocketed over the bumps.

'Shut it down, shut it down!' I yelled, realising that in front of us was a wire fence that would slice us like a hot knife through butter.

Dad hit the magneto switches, killing the engine, and we rolled to a stop. I was shaking from the adrenalin rush following those terrifying few seconds, berating Dad for almost killing us—not that it was his fault. At least the steering lever worked at high speed!

With the modifications on the trike complete, I took it back to

Porepunkah to test them out with Steve. The throttle control worked perfectly, but I spent a few hours practising taxiing with the steering lever as this was difficult to do with my left hand while I held the wing level with my right; normally a two-handed job for anyone.

The idea was for me to line up the trike down the centre of the runway with a bit of speed, then when I was going straight, I'd take my hand off the steering lever and lock it on the base-bar adaptation—the castered design of the front wheel would in theory keep it tracking straight. Now having control of the wing with both hands, I would apply full power and take off. Not a problem! In still air it worked fine, but later I would face serious complications in windy conditions.

One thing I hadn't had converted were the brakes, which were operated by a foot pedal. I had discussed it with Steve, concluding that they weren't necessary considering it was a big airfield with little traffic. Given that we were landing on grass, the trike slowed down quite quickly anyway.

However, early one morning as I finished preparing myself for a quick flying session before the thermals kicked in, with Steve in the back, I started the engine to warm it up. I'm not sure what happened but the engine throttled up, and suddenly we were heading straight for the hangar at a running pace. I fumbled to put my hand in the steering lever, but there was nowhere to go except straight. By the time Steve turned off the magneto switches, shutting the engine down, we were metres from the hangar. All I could do was brace myself, hoping it wasn't going to hurt. 'Shiiit!' I said through gritted teeth as we rammed into the side of the hangar, bouncing off.

All I could think was, *Oh no, I've blown it! What a dumb mistake.* I just hoped Steve wouldn't have second thoughts about teaching me to fly.

'You all right?' he asked, appearing not particularly fazed by the event.

Apart from the dent in the door of the hangar, there didn't seem to be any damage. However, when we tried to push the trike back to turn it around, we realised the fibreglass fairing on the pod had been pushed back, jamming the front wheel.

Steve stuck his head down to survey the damage. 'We can fix that,' he said optimistically.

He took the brackets off, bent them back in his workshop at home, and I was back in business flying the next morning. I decided to get the brake modified after that.

With the trike fully adapted I felt free, able to use all the controls. I practised my turns, flying straight, controlling the throttle on landings with Steve talking me through; he only took over when it looked as if things were going a bit pear-shaped. I was now ready to get stuck into my training to become a pilot.

I had two weeks off work in mid-February and hoped to complete my pilot's certificate in that time.

I flew early mornings and late afternoons when it was cooler and less thermic, with theory in between. The thermals would start to kick in by 10.30 a.m. and wouldn't stop until about 5 p.m., so we avoided this period as the trike, with such a large wing area, made flying in thermals like riding a big roller coaster: scary and very hard work.

Steve took me through the paces, following mountain ridge lines which was a lot of fun, spiral descents, engine failures, cross-country flights to airfields in other valleys, unaided landings with the engine idling and under power—all of which I picked up very quickly, with Steve giving advice and encouragement from the back seat. But the one thing I struggled with was emergency landings. As the ground came up to meet the aircraft, I would push the base-bar forward to flare (reduce the air speed and descent rate of the aircraft) too late or too early, and we'd end up bouncing or landing too hard. Steve wanted me to have another session that afternoon, so during my break I did some visualisation exercises to try and get it right in my mind, then have a snooze to refresh myself.

It was hot at the airfield at 5 p.m. Steve took over throttling the engine for my emergency landing practice. Once in the air around thirty feet or so he'd put the throttle to idle, the nose would drop, I'd pull the bar in to increase speed, and at the last moment push the bar forward to flare and hopefully kiss the ground instead of thumping. Up and down, up and down we went, fitting in three landings on the length of runway.

The first run was the same as before: terrible bouncing or pancaking. I was getting so frustrated, and so was Steve, going by the impatience in his voice. But on the third run, something happened, and it just clicked; I greased each one in on the following two runs.

'I think you can go solo tonight,' said Steve as we pulled up to the hangar.

'Ah ... really, solo, tonight?' I said, my stomach tightening.

I had expected to take most of the two weeks of practice before going solo; by then it had only been four days.

'It's going to be a perfect still evening—you'll be fine. I will be on the radio talking you through it,' said Steve.

Lisa, Steve's wife, also an instructor, echoed her confidence in my ability.

'Tonight it is, then!' I said.

At 7 p.m. the harshness of the daylight was beginning to fade, with Mt Buffalo's soft veil blanketing the airfield. The evening was ideal, not a breath of wind, only the smell of dry grass in the warm air.

Mark, a recent student, refuelled my plane. 'It's a perfect night, Dave, just like when I did my solo, hey, Steve? You're going to love it when you're up!' he remarked, giving me encouragement and calming my nerves.

'How are you feeling, Dave?' asked Lisa, her video camera extending from one eye.

'A little nervous.'

'In my seventeen years of teaching students, everyone is nervous,' Steve said.

'How are you feeling, Steve?' Lisa asked, turning the camera to him.

'Nervous, ha-ha!' Mark said, having a giggle.

Without Steve in the back seat, Mark fastened in a forty-litre water container to act as ballast.

'You'll be lighter, so don't use full power on take-off,' Steve advised.

'OK, got it.'

Taxiing up the side of the runway, I remembered my first flight the previous Easter, ten months ago. At the time, taxiing with Steve, my dream of flying solo was only an idea; now I was on my own, about to make my dream a reality.

To be honest, while I was excited, I was also shitting myself a tad. I was so used to having Steve in the back as my bit of insurance; if anything went wrong, he would get me out of trouble. Now it was all up to me.

As I went through the pre-flight checklist that I had done many times before, I settled in and started to feel more comfortable. Taking a deep breath to settle my nerves and relax, I gave the call on the radio to the other air traffic: 'Porepunkah traffic Microlight 2526, entering runway 05, Porepunkah.'

It's now or never, I thought, throttling up and turning onto the runway, lining up the trike down the centre. The engine roared and within seconds I blasted off, climbing higher and higher, the hangars, Steve, Lisa and Mark disappearing below me. The air was warm and smooth; passing through pockets of cooler air and back into the warmth was a marvellous sensation. The higher I climbed, the brighter the daylight became as I moved out of the shadow of Mt Buffalo.

As I headed over to Bright in the next valley, my nerves settled. It was so peaceful to be by myself; I felt relaxed and was relishing the moment. I called Steve on the radio to let him know my position, but the mountain blocked the signal; I could only hear the other pilots buzzing around Mt Buffalo. I wasn't worried as the plan was to fly to Bright then come back in about half an hour. I was on track.

Lisa's video showed how pleased Steve was that he'd got me to the stage of flying solo. It was a huge credit to him, for his willingness to take a chance on me. But I later learned that he was somewhat nervous until I came back into radio range.

As I headed back to the airfield, to my right above I noticed two trikes buzzing along the ridge line of a mountain, looking like little mosquitos in the setting sun.

With no wind, I decided to do a straight-in approach, lining up the runway from three miles out. Steve may not have been behind me in the back seat, but I could hear his voice running me through the checks: 'Check the wind sock, keep the bar in for speed, flare at the very last minute.' I was a little high and in hindsight probably should have done a circuit, but with a couple of sweeping turns I lost enough height. On glide approach, with the engine on idle, the aircraft floated down, then a few feet above the ground I pushed the bar forward to flare and kissed the ground gently, pulling off one of my best landings.

I was exhilarated, filled with pure happiness, as I taxied back, rolling to a stop. It was the most exciting and scariest experience of my life. I had done it; I had achieved my dream, and within only 17.55 hours of flying time.

Steve rushed up to shake my hand, congratulating me. 'Oh man, what a legend!' he said, laughing; he was as happy as I was that

I'd finally done it. Steve and Lisa cracked a bottle of champagne, and we celebrated in the warm evening as the pink hue of the setting sun faded around us.

With ten more days at Bright, I built up my hours, increasing my skill level, getting a better understanding of the aircraft and my limitations, and completing my cross-country endorsement. Flying in the early mornings and late afternoon each day, Steve took me through more theory and I did the exams in the middle of the day when it was hot and thermic. It was full on. After two weeks of 4 a.m. starts, followed by study and flying each day, I was well and truly done.

I hadn't given my achievement much thought from the perspective of an 'aviation first' in Australia, if not the world, until ABC radio requested an interview and *The Border Mail* came down for a story and photo shoot of my triumph. Whether it was a 'first' or not made no difference to me; all I'd wanted to do was fly.

Following the newspaper interview, Steve turned to me and said, 'So Dave, what's next?'

I thought about it for a moment. That I had achieved my dream was still sinking in. I had achieved what others thought was impossible. I now wanted to do something bigger, something that would test me, something that would push me to my absolute limits. Whatever it was, it had to take me out of my comfort zone and into the unknown—an ultimate challenge to really find out what my six percent was capable of.

'Flying solo around Australia would be good!' I said.

Steve laughed, patting me on the back. 'Oh man! That'd be some trip!'

35

AFTER SOLO

There are moments in life when our achievements become our personal victories.

A few weeks after getting back from Bright, I attended the monthly microlight club meeting. Barry and Mike, whom I first met at the 2005 airshow the previous year, were there, as was Mark from the night of my first solo, with whom I'd become good friends.

Wheeling out, I ran into Jim. 'Hi, David,' he said.

'Oh, hi Jim,' I said, surprised, as I hadn't expected to see him there.

'Congratulations. That's a really great effort, well done!' he said.

I appreciated his generous congratulations, but I really wanted to yell out, 'I told you so!' I had proven him and my other detractors wrong, achieving 'the impossible.' As Paul Keating said after winning the unwinnable 1993 election: 'This is the sweetest victory of all!' It was certainly a sweet victory for me, but it also opened the door for other people in similar situations who wanted to fly.

Few people understand quadriplegia. Simply mentioning the word conjures many false and limited ideas of a person's potential. For Jim, taking on the challenge of teaching me to fly, without understanding my disability and what I could do, may have been too overwhelming—too risky, even too scary.

But just because someone doesn't think you can do something does not mean it can't be done. It is only their opinion, based on their limited knowledge and experience, so you don't need to accept it. If people never tried because it went against what others thought, we'd still believe the earth is flat, the Wright Brothers would never have achieved powered flight, and we wouldn't have deep-fried Mars Bars.

A lot of people have low expectations of what people with disabilities can achieve, thereby creating barriers for those who want to challenge the norm. Generally speaking, I don't think this is out of malice or discrimination, but rather a lack of knowledge or understanding. And these obstacles of perception aren't limited to people with disabilities; it can extend to race, sex, religion—you name it.

Having dealt with these attitudes over the years—whether it was studying, getting a job or just buying clothes—I eventually reached a tipping point when my dream of flying was threatened, which motivated me to crush the barrier once and for all.

With my sights set on one of the biggest goals of my life—to fly solo around Australia—I wanted it to be much more than a personal challenge. I wanted to show that people with disabilities can do so much more than what many people assume is possible.

My vision for the flight was to change attitudes and raise the public's expectations of what people with disabilities can achieve.

I hope that when someone in the community meets a person with a disability, they may be a little more open-minded and consider who they are as a person and what they might be capable of. Not be quick to judge and give them a go.

36

FINAL THOUGHTS

What will I be capable of with just six percent? This thought had been swirling around my mind since I was told what level of function I had left. Having never met anyone with my level of disability, I had no benchmark, no idea of what I would be capable of. I had to rely on what a few doctors could tell me: 'You should be able to push a wheelchair on flat ground, and you might even be able to drive again.'

I constantly wondered what my level of disability equated to in quality of life. With six percent of my muscles working, would I achieve only six percent of what was possible prior to my accident? Did it mean my life would be six percent fulfilling? Or did it mean something else?

The day I worked out how to get myself into bed on my own was the day I knew that six percent was only a number, and that a person's functional ability had no bearing on a person's true potential. Someone with more function might be able to do more physically, but it did not mean he or she would end up achieving more.

A person's potential is limited far more by what we think is possible than by a physical disability or any other challenge. By thinking outside of the square, by doing it differently, we can overcome obstacles and achieve far more than we ever imagined.

Doing it differently means having an open mind, being creative and exploring various solutions to navigate problems.

It is about having a go. Instead of saying, 'I can't,' say 'Maybe I can!' and then work towards your goal.

Another key ingredient is perseverance, which I believe is the most important factor in achieving our goals. If we have the emotional stamina to keep going, we can transform what may have seemed impossible into being possible. This is what allows us to be our best, to strive towards our true potential.

It was one thing to have the motivation and desire to chase a goal, but having others' support was fundamental to me achieving far more than I could have done alone. Their support, whether emotional or physical, helped remove obstacles that could have stopped me from achieving my dreams, from doing my best. Everyone—disabled or not—needs support from others. I have been very fortunate to have such a great family who have supported me constantly and held up a lantern at the end of a very long tunnel in some of my darkest moments, especially in my early days following my accident. This support has also come from the many people who have entered my life, including my wife, Linda, in later years, friends, carers, Steve Ruffels, the nurses and doctors in hospital and rehab, work colleagues, teammates and many, many others. I could never have achieved what I have done without all those people in my life.

A final thought: while setting goals and working hard to achieve them is paramount to having a fulfilling life, of equal importance are the experiences we have along the way. The joy, the pain, the highs and lows, our successes and failures—all of it makes us who we are.

I have no regrets about the cards life has dealt me. I am truly grateful for all the experiences in my life journey, as these have made me who I am and enabled me to glimpse the potential that each of us has within us.

EPILOGUE

'I'm going to fly solo around Australia!' These words rolled off my tongue very easily. It was only when I unfolded one of twenty-nine World Aeronautical Charts and plotted how far I could fly in good conditions in one day that the enormity of the task began to sink in.

With less than sixty hours flying time before my first long cross-country flight in 2007, you could say that I was a little naive to the challenges I would face flying around Australia. I didn't know that the preparation and planning would consume my life as I dealt with the highs and lows, trying to make it a reality.

When my support team and I finally set off on the flight in 2013, the challenge was not only physical but mental as we dealt with weather, fatigue and mechanical problems.

The flight pushed me to the edge of my limits, and I discovered what flying solo really meant when my life was on the line.

My second book, *On a Wing and a Chair*, tells the story of this adventure, and how I achieved a world first: becoming the first person with quadriplegia to fly solo around Australia.

ACKNOWLEDGEMENTS

A special thanks to Darrell Pitt for mentoring me through my writing journey. Your patience while listening to my rambling, and guidance with ideas and inspiration to keep plugging away, is greatly appreciated. I think I still owe you a lunch!

To my wife, Linda: thank you for your ongoing love and support over the six years it has taken me to complete this book, and for your encouragement while listening to my repetitive reflection; it helped turn my thoughts into a story that I'm proud of.

I would like to thank my dad, Brian, for straightening out my tenses, grammar and paragraph structure in an early draft and for the final proofread. I also appreciate your instructions about prepositions—now I know what they are used for … or is it, 'for what they are to be used'?

A big thanks to Tanya Carter for your friendship, for going easy on me with feedback and help with marketing ideas; you were tremendous. Thanks to Andrew Raszevski for a great cover photo of me and working your magic on all my old photos; they look so much better. Also, many thanks to Karen Rumley from I.D.Yours for producing the wonderful illustrations from my dodgy sketches and photos; they're awesome.

Thanks to Nadine Davidoff: your insightful guidance and skilled copy editing has made my story shine.

And finally, I would like to acknowledge my family for their unwavering love and support; thanks also to my friends and everyone who has been part of my life in so many ways. Each of you has played a role and given me a story to tell: cheers!

www.ingramcontent.com/pod-product-compliance
Lightning Source LLC
Chambersburg PA
CBHW032030290426
44110CB00012B/741